TRAINING FOR

PERSONAL SAFETY

AT WORK

TRAINING FOR

PERSONAL SAFETY

AT WORK

by
Chris Cardy

in association with Diana Lamplugh OBE

Gower
for The Suzy Lamplugh Trust

First published by
Gower Publishing Company Limited
Gower House
Croft Road
Aldershot
Hants GU11 3HR
England

Gower Publishing Company Limited
Old Post Road
Brookfield
Vermont 05036
USA

This paperback edition published 1995
Reprinted 1996

CIP catalogue records for this book are available from the British Library.

ISBN 0 566 07680 2 Paperback
    1 85904 048 4 Looseleaf

Printed by Watkiss Studios Limited, Biggleswade, Beds SG18 9ST

Contents

List of figures vii

Acknowledgements ix

Introduction by Diana Lamplugh OBE 1

How to use these materials 7

PART ONE   RESOURCE MATERIALS 11

1   Defining violence and aggression 12

2   The risks in perspective 15
- Research findings 15
- The risk of crime 22

3   Employer and employee roles 30

4   Identifying risks at work 35
- Where to investigate 36
- Investigation methods 40
- Other methods 46

5   Developing policy and procedures 48
- The policy document 49
- Implementing policy – developing procedures 52

6   Reporting violent incidents 54

7   Aftercare – helping and supporting victims 59
- Debriefing 59
- Counselling 60
- Visiting victims 60
- Time off work 61
- Protected earnings 61
- Legal help 61
- Other staff 62

8   Taking control 63
- Fear 63
- Anger 64
- Stress 66
- Tension 69
- Relaxation – tension control 71

9   Communication – assertiveness 80
- Aggressive behaviour 80
- Learning to be assertive 87

v

10	Workwise – good practice guide	98
	• Travelling	98
	• Reception areas/waiting rooms	104
	• Access to the workplace	106
	• The environs of the workplace	107
	• Interviewing	108
	• Other people's homes	110
	• Other people's premises	112
	• Patterns of work	113
	• Handling money or valuables	113
	• Working from home or at home	116
11	In the event	118
	• Coping with violence	118
12	Non-verbal communication	127
	• Recognizing signals	127
13	Helping yourself – recognizing and avoiding danger	135
	• Self-awareness	135
	• Awareness of others	138
	• Awareness of the environment	141
	PART TWO GUIDELINES FOR TRAINERS	143
	• The trainer's role	145
	• Values and beliefs	146
	• Adult learners	148
	• Identifying training needs	149
	• Aims and learning objectives	150
	• Motivating learners	151
	• Planning training	152
	• Presenting training	154
	• Training aids	156
	• Training methods	157
	• Evaluating training	159
	PART THREE SAMPLE TRAINING PROGRAMMES	161
	• Introduction to violence at work	163
	• The manager's role in preventing violence at work – an introduction	167
	• Looking after yourself – tension and relaxation	171
	• Coping with violence	175
	• Communication skills	181
	• Developing policy and procedures to combat violence at work	185
	• Practical steps to safety	192
	PART FOUR REFERENCES	197
	• Books and booklets	199
	• Articles	201
	• Reports and papers	203
	• Training resources	205
	• Organizations	207

List of figures

2.1	Violence to staff in the health services	16
2.2	Violence against teachers in one week	17
2.3	Violence against DSS staff	17
2.4–2.8	Violence against the public services	19–21
2.9	Attacks on Tesco staff	22
2.10	The timing of violent incidents	23
2.11	Assaults on London Underground staff	23
2.12	Street crime	24
2.13	The increase in crime	25
2.14	Increases in car crime	25
2.15	The rise in violent crime	25
2.16	Types of crime	26
2.17	Breakdown of sexual offences	27
2.18	The statistics on rape	28
2.19	At what age are you most at risk from rape?	28
3.1	Personal safety in the workplace	33

Acknowledgements

By Chris Cardy

I should like to express my thanks to my colleagues at The Local Government Management Board for their help, advice, ideas and support; to Diana Lamplugh whose idea it was and who, having badgered me into doing it, provided ideas, support and raw materials and became a good friend; The Health and Safety Executive, particularly Mary McAleese, for 'technical' advice and reading the final draft; to the Home Office and Hendon Police College for information and advice; to Celia Piper of Piper Hastings and Co.; to Mary Harvey of Harvey Training Ltd. and Marina Murphy, Independent Consultant, for reading and commenting; and to my long-suffering husband Peter, for his help, reading and commenting on drafts and putting up with 'violence' for the last year!

By The Suzy Lamplugh Trust

The Suzy Lamplugh Trust is greatly indebted to Chris Cardy for all her work on this manual which she has generously donated to the Trust: all the author's royalties in respect of this manual are paid to the Trust to help continue its important work.

The Trust is also grateful to the Publishers for the help which they have given in connection with this manual.

Foreword

Since this excellent Resource Manual was published in 1992, the demand for copies has steadily increased. Unfortunately this is not surprising.

Workplace crime has become a major issue and many of these crimes have involved violence to staff. The annual incidents reported in the British Crime Survey is around 350,000. Considering the whole spectrum of the HSE definition of violence and aggression, this figure is bound to be an under-estimation.

Fortunately, the legal regulations have extended beyond Section 2(1) of the Health and Safety at Work Act 1974, with the 1993 EC Directives. Risk Assessment is an explicit duty under the Management of Health and Safety at Work Regulations 1992.

All employers need to follow up their risk assessments with appropriate preventative and protective measures and management arrangements (e.g. planning, organisation, control, monitoring and review). They must give employees adequate information and training to be able to understand the risks and the measures (including procedures, policies etc.) taken to deal with them.

Once these have been tried and agreed in consultation with employees and, whenever possible their union representatives, it is then the employees responsibility not to put themselves in danger, or their colleagues, or their workplace. Employees who deliberately ignore the procedures and policies for health and safety might be considered negligent should an accident occur.

However if some employers are deemed to have failed in their legal duty to take care of their staff, it is the employer's negligence which could be in question. Moreover if employers suffer incidents without any sign of action, they will certainly attract scrutiny from Health and Safety Regulators.

Also, as more employees are beginning to consider claims against their employers as a result of the reduction in the level of compensation under the Criminal Injuries Compensation Board, insurers will certainly back up the HSE regulations. Employers must ensure that violence at work is integrated with their other health and safety responsibilities.

The Trust has continued to extend its work to enable all employers to carry through their duties. In November 1994 the Trust published Guidance for Employers, "Violence and Aggression at Work; Reducing the Risks - Policy, Principles and Practice." This contains all the up-to-date information from the HSE, is endorsed by the CBI and was prepared with members of HSE's Committee on Violence to Staff, including the TUC and Industrial Society.

No changes have been needed to the text of this Resource Manual. Chris Cardy's 'bible' on the subject is proven and still an invaluable asset for every employer.

The Trust has a number of other training resources specifically for personal safety at work, including booklets for employees, videos, and training courses.

Diana Lamplugh OBE
4th November, 1994

FACING THE FACTS

Aggression and violence in the workplace is a growing problem. At one extreme, figures issued by the Metropolitan Police indicate that during 1991 in Greater London, for instance, bank robberies increased by 83.7 per cent (294 in the period January–November); and building society robberies by 5 per cent (480 in the same period).

However, another aspect of this problem is seen in the effect of the current recession as threatened closures, reduced budgets and redundancies affect not only those directly involved but also everyone who is even remotely connected. Insecurity, loss of confidence and control increase the stress, tension and consequent lack of objectivity and over-sensitivity.

Between these two ends of the spectrum there can be few places of work which can have escaped the daily effects of aggression in at least one of its many forms.

WHY CARE?

All employers have a legal duty under Section 2 (1) of the Health and Safety at Work Act 1974 to ensure, so far as is reasonably practicable, the health, safety and welfare at work of their employees. This duty extends to the personal protection of employees; it can indeed become a criminal offence for an employer to neglect it. However, the benefits of developing an effective policy for preventing and dealing with violence at work extend beyond any statutory requirement.

The severe personal and organizational costs associated with violence at work are compelling reasons for attempting to eradicate it from the workplace. There are obvious costs associated with litigation against the employer and the resulting media publicity, compensation costs, higher insurance premiums and time off work due to physical injury.

In addition, there are the hidden but equally real costs arising from emotional stress. This may be manifested in physical symptoms, absenteeism, staff turnover, low productivity, and reduced job involvement and satisfaction. Low staff morale and a poor organizational image clearly contribute to difficulties in recruiting and retaining staff.

Obviously physical attacks are dangerous and can result in injury, disability, or even death. They also cause stress and anxiety. Similarly, serious or persistent verbal abuse and threats affect both individual effectiveness and morale. The costs of inaction with respect to violence at work and the personal, monetary and organizational benefits of effective action to combat violence cannot be underestimated.

RESEARCH

The findings of research by Phillips, Stockdale and Joeman for The Suzy Lamplugh Trust in 'The Risks in Going to Work' with the London School of Economics (published in 1989) concluded that:

- Violence at work is an issue for both employers and employees.
- It is widespread – not confined to 'women's work' or to the UK.
- Perceptions of risk do not always match reality.
- Anxiety is no substitute for action. Institutional provision is crucial to employees' safety – all too often action only follows a serious incident.
- Violence at work has high costs to both the individual and the organization.
- Young males are the group most vulnerable to physical attack in the course of work.

PRACTICAL PERSPECTIVES

1. Aggression and violence in the workplace is a people problem – *not* a gender problem – at least twice as many men as women suffer from assaults every year (and men are much less likely to report them).

2. If women are seen as a special need as far as violence and aggression are concerned, it is also likely that men will ignore their own problems with aggression as well as their attitudes and needs. They will continue to think of women as inferior instead of equal though different. Many of the external problems will also go unchallenged.

3. Men and women need to be assumed to have equal but different problems with aggression and violence. They need to have those problems without stigma, condemnation or surprise.

4. Violence is not defined as solely assault, attack and rape; verbal abuse, sexual and racial harassment, bullying, innuendo and even deliberate silence can be the triggers which escalate a situation into something worse.

5. Even if the escalation does not take place and there is no overt aggression, most people are so badly affected by covert aggression that they feel, and therefore become, more vulnerable. Fear is very debilitating and can result in behaviour which presents vulnerability – muggers mug 'push-overs', i.e. easy targets (once again the under-reporting is by men). Only bulliable people are bullied.

2

6. The majority of incidents occur when people are out and about: at, to or from work or during their daily lives. The most likely timing is late afternoon when the schools come out and the pubs close! (Once again most attacks are between men aged 16–25.) Eighty-five per cent of muggings on the London Underground are perpetrated by men on men. (Most attacks on women are by people they know. Most rapes occur in the home or on first dates.)

7. To be really effective, procedures, physical danger points and structural changes need to be considered by both employer and employee.

WHY A TRAINER PACK?

A principal aim of The Suzy Lamplugh Trust is to reduce aggression and violence at work. The Suzy Lamplugh Trust believes that consideration and care by employers for their employees improves not only the transaction between members of the public and the employees but also the transaction between the organization and its staff. This has proved to lead to better cooperation, loyalty and identification with the consequence of less stress-related absence and illness.

However, while it is true that the employers have a statutory duty to provide a safe and healthy workplace, employees also have a duty to take reasonable care of their own health and safety and for those who may be affected by their actions.

The Suzy Lamplugh Trust believes that personal safety for those at work involves cooperation, coordination and mutual goodwill. It is cost-effective for employers to look after their staff. However many employers still regard the topic as inappropriate to their workplace. Some even fear that taking any action at all will unnecessarily raise anxiety.

This Trainer's Resource Pack is highly recommended. When I first read the contents my reaction was the same time and time again: 'I wish I'd thought of that!' All trainers, whether they have many years of experience, are weighed down with qualifications or have been forced into the job simply because 'they are there', or have a vague responsibility for health and safety, can find everything that they could wish for in this pack in order to construct a course on enabling staff to deal with, defuse, or cope with, avoid and be aware of aggression and violence and its ramifications in whatever area of work they are involved.

Chris Cardy has done a splendid job. The Suzy Lamplugh Trust is delighted that this aid to personal safety for all employees will now, through Gower, be available to everyone.

DO YOU RECOGNIZE ANY OF THE FOLLOWING SCENARIOS?

Before you start using this resource manual, you might like to check your current awareness of the problems of personal safety, violence and aggression at work, and that of your employees.

Sexual harassment or blackmail?

A debt collector visiting a flat on a housing estate was met by the sight of an attractive scantily dressed woman draped on the settee watching a pornographic video with overloud sound. Taken aback by this scene he backed out and failed to collect the money.

Overt aggression

One of the occupants of a block of flats continually made complaints, the latest of which was about the overflow of his sink. He rang up repeatedly and was always told that the telephonist would 'pass the message on'. Being a man of brute strength but few words, the man one day reached the end of his tether. He ripped the sink from the wall and carried it down to the housing department. 'What' he shouted to the young temporary receptionist, 'are you going to do about this?' And he plonked the sink down on her desk.

'It says here', the girl replied, 'that you cannot come without an appointment', and pointing to the offending sink she said, 'Please remove this object and bring it back on Monday'. 'I bloody won't', he yelled and picking it up he hurled it at the wall with such force that fragments ricocheted around the open plan office hurting several people and causing some damage.

Invasion of personal space

On returning to his office, the solicitor finds his client using the 'phone and writing on his desk pad. Hearing the door open, the client turns round, and calmly tears off his note. 'I asked them to put my calls through here; hope you don't mind', says the client. The solicitor feels growing indignation.

Straight into trouble

The child psychologist told to investigate a possible case of child abuse goes in the evening to visit a flat on a run-down housing estate in the hope of meeting both the parents and the child. The place is ill-lit but she decides to wait with the mother until the father returns with his friends from the pub. She has let no one know where she is, there is no telephone and she finds herself trapped in a high-rise flat.

Without protective procedures

Many people were aware just how desperate the man who was threatened with eviction could be. He had a gun, he made threats, he had a history of problems. When the bailiff arrived, the man was trapped in a no-win situation and shot the bailiff in full camera view of the media.

How would you or your staff have handled situations such as these? Would you have recognized them all as threats? This training manual is designed to help your organization recognize potential threats to the safety of your staff and to help your staff develop the personal skills they need to avoid dangerous situations or, if faced with them, handle them safely.

Diana Lamplugh OBE
10 April 1992

The Suzy Lamplugh Trust
14 East Sheen Avenue
London SW14 8AS

How to use these materials

These materials aim to provide trainers with a resource that will enable them to design, plan and provide training to promote safer working practices within their organizations.

The materials are designed for use by trainers who are not experts in terms of the content, i.e. violence at work and promoting safe working practices, but who have skills, experience or interests in providing learning opportunities for people in this subject.

While providing resources for a range of training activities this material/pack does not claim to have the answer to every question; nor will it solve problems. People themselves will have to do that by implementing the learning from the materials.

Far from being prescriptive, the materials are designed as a resource to enable informed decision making about training initiatives and activities that will suit particular circumstances. Thus they do not provide an 'off-the-shelf' response to every need in every different organizational context.

Clearly the materials cannot do the job of a trainer, but they do provide resources based on research, in one place, in a usable form, and ideas of how the resources can be used to provide training programmes. Trainers will still need to read and get to know the contents of Part One in particular, be clear about training needs in their own situation, plan, design and run training events (perhaps using the sample programmes in Part Three) and evaluate the training.

PART ONE

The first part of the materials provides the coverage of the subject of safety from violence at work. It is divided into sections, each of which deals with a particular aspect. Wherever possible it is written using checklists and key points for clarity and simplicity. The content can be used in a number of ways. For example:

- you may choose to read it as a whole to get an overview of what is covered so that in planning and designing training you have a 'feel' for what is available;

7

- the sections are self-contained and can be used separately if you wish to incorporate a particular aspect of the content into a training event;

- the sections can be used individually to develop lecture notes, handouts and so on if this is what you need;

- a section could be used by particular groups depending on their role and task, for example managers could be provided with the material on 'developing policies and procedures' as a follow-up to training or you could use the section as the basis for taking them through the process; or a health and safety group could use 'identifying risks' as a guide in the task of actually designing an investigation; a particular staff group could have the material from 'Workwise' on interviewing as a follow-up guide or reminder after training;

- the checklists and keypoints within the sections can be used to develop handouts or overhead projector transparencies or written up on flipcharts in training sessions.

Part One is thus intended to be used in many different ways and adapted to suit individual needs and circumstances in very different organizational contexts.

Part One takes its particular form because training and learning is not necessarily about running training programmes in the sense of formal 'off-the-job' events. The materials could be used 'on the job' with 'at risk' groups (for example, receptionists); as part of meetings, for example with managers, persuading them of their role and responsibilities in policy development; or with health and safety committees to help them to perform their role in providing advice or information. The materials can also be used as a basis for notes or guidelines where formal training is not an option but providing information is.

PART TWO

This part of the package is concerned with the trainer's role and the process of providing training rather than with the content of that training, i.e. the 'how' rather than the 'what' of the training.

It is not intended here to teach experienced trainers to 'suck eggs' but to provide guidelines as reminders or triggers for action in key areas, for example when the trainer is:

- relatively new to training or inexperienced;

- new to this potentially sensitive subject which can arouse personal or emotional responses;

- unused to training which has wider organizational and policy implications within the workplace as well as implications for individual performance;

- new to the content and wishing to concentrate on that while using the checklists to ensure attention is paid to all parts of the process;

- working with a co-trainer when the checklists can be used to ensure there is an understood and agreed process throughout for which the individuals take responsibility.

8

PART THREE

The sample training programmes in Part Three are just that, samples designed to show ways in which the contents of Part One can be used and the types of training events you could provide. Some trainers may be able to take them and use them almost as they are but many will want to adapt or amend them significantly. In other cases trainers could simply lift the exercises and activities from various programmes to construct something to meet their own specific needs.

PART FOUR

The reference section contains not only information about reading and other training materials but also details of sources of further help, advice and information.

PART ONE

RESOURCE MATERIALS

1
Defining Violence and Aggression

We very often speak of violence and aggression as if we are perfectly clear about what they are. We forget that individual perceptions of violence and aggression differ. We also often assume that there is some shared, readily understood concept of such behaviour as well as common knowledge of the scale of violence and aggression at work and elsewhere.

Reactions to violence and aggression vary, from people who do not acknowledge it as a problem in their job, neighbourhood or society to people who are afraid to step outside their own front door. Media reports bring violent and aggressive incidents to our attention, and we often hear or read of the increasing violence of our society.

What is it that we are all talking about?

It is difficult to be precise, to define words like violence and aggression because of perceptual differences, and much research work stresses this problem. Dictionary definitions focus on the words and what they mean in an objective, academic sense. They tell us something of what is generally understood by the words themselves and what they are used to mean. However, such definitions tell us nothing of the causes or effects of aggression and violence; nor how to recognize either in an organizational or work context.

In order to try to encapsulate meaning there have been attempts to produce 'working' definitions and these generally seek to describe the behavioural characteristics associated with aggression and violence and their effects.

Some examples of 'working' definitions follow:

- Any incident in which an employee is abused, threatened or assaulted by a member of the public in circumstances arising out of the course of his or her employment. (Health and Safety Executive's working definition of violence 1989)

- The application of force, severe threat or serious abuse by members of the public towards people arising out of the course of their work whether or not they are on duty. This includes severe verbal abuse or threat where this is judged likely to turn into actual violence; serious or persistent harassment (including racial or sexual harassment); threat with a weapon; major or minor injuries; fatalities. (DSS, 'Violence to Staff: Report of DSS Advisory Committee on Violence to Staff', 1988)

- Behaviour which produces damaging or hurtful effects, physically or emotionally, on people. (ADSS, 'Guidelines and Recommendations to Employers on Violence against Employees in the Personal Social Services', 1987)

These working definitions widen the dictionary definitions to encompass verbal aggression or abuse, threat or harassment. They also attempt to describe the behaviour associated with aggression and violence as well as its effects on the victim. Although some working definitions deal specifically with behaviour from the public most are wide enough to take into account that the public would include business contacts, contractors, service providers and others with whom an organization does business. In addition, though not directly mentioned, there remains the possibility of aggressive or violent behaviour from colleagues within the workplace.

Seeking a definition may seem rather pedantic but it is an important, if often forgotten, basic step in addressing problems of aggression and violence at work for these reasons:

1. We need to know what it is we are talking about and trying to deal with. Many people still assume violence only includes serious physical attack, rape and murder. In practice a wide range of behaviour is now recognized as violent or aggressive and appreciated as being damaging to individual employees and the work of the organization. The range of behaviour includes:

Physical violence
- assault causing death
- assault causing serious physical injury
- minor injuries
- kicking
- biting
- punching
- use of weapons
- use of missiles
- spitting
- scratching
- sexual assault

Non-physical violence
- verbal abuse
- racial or sexual abuse
- threats – with or without weapons
- physical posturing
- threatening gestures
- abusive 'phone calls
- threatening use of dogs
- harassment in all forms
- swearing
- shouting
- name calling
- bullying
- insults
- innuendo
- deliberate silence

2. Developing a definition should take into account the context and culture of the organization and the characteristics of the employees and the potential aggressors. For example:

   - children, in school or in care, may use verbal abuse or minor assaults as a result of temper or letting off steam;

   - a mentally ill patient may not be capable of making rational judgements about behaviour and could lash out verbally or physically;

   - people in places of entertainment or pubs may swear as a result of high spirits and alcohol in some cases and present no threat.

   Considering the contextual issues in developing a definition helps to ensure that it is workable because it encompasses what the organization (employers and employees) believes to be violent behaviour as opposed to behaviour resulting from other factors.

3. Perceptions of aggression and violence will vary between victims and non-victims and between people at high risk and people at much less risk. Not everyone will be equally vulnerable or resilient when it comes to dealing with violence or the fear of it. A process of involving people in working towards a definition brings a variety of experiences, views and perceptions into the open so that they can be taken into account in developing a definition to which everyone can subscribe.

13

4. A definition, although artificial in some ways, can be shared, explained and under-stood, thereby establishing a basis for recognizing violence as such. General under-standing can significantly increase people's willingness to report incidents. Under-reporting of incidents has been a serious problem that many believe results from a lack of confidence that reports of violence will be perceived by others as the victim perceives them. The dismissing of reports as 'part of the job' or the over-sensitivity of the victim has been all too common.

Developing a working definition of aggression and violence for the organization is therefore an important foundation of understanding upon which to build commitment, policy, procedures and working practices.

It does not matter if someone else's definition is used as a starting point or the process is begun with a blank sheet of paper. Whether the choice is to define aggressive behaviour and violent behaviour separately, or use violence as a term to cover a continuum of behaviour, as many organizations do, is not critical.

Nor does it matter whether the definition sounds learned or is a straightforward list of behaviour included within the definition.

What does matter is that the definition is developed in such a way that it is shared and so can inform the future behaviour and perceptions of everyone. This implies consulta-tion with the workforce, specifically those people most likely to be at risk, rather than the imposition of a definition by policy makers, managers or others relatively remote from the 'front line'.

This process may appear a long-winded and time-consuming way of arriving at a form of words but it is well worth doing as it can cover a good deal of the groundwork necessary to develop a policy (see Chapter 5)

Finally, within these materials 'violence' is used as an all-embracing term and is defined as:

any behaviour towards an employee in the course of his or her work that has damaging physical or psychological effects upon that person.

The definition includes all forms of physical and non-physical abuse, attack, threat or assault and is intended to be victim-centred in that the assessment of what is damaging, particularly psychologically, must come from the victim him- or herself.

2
The Risks in Perspective

The high profile reporting of incidents of violence and the increased awareness of employers and employees of the risks at work are both positive and negative.

They are positive because we all need to be aware of risks inherent in our life and work if we are to develop safe practices. They are negative because such knowledge and awareness can engender fear of violence that is out of all proportion to the risk. In assessing the risks we face we need to consider evidence from a range of sources, as well as looking critically at our own working environment and practices, if we are to have a balanced view.

RESEARCH FINDINGS

During the 1980s the rise in the number of assaults of various kinds on employees in the course of their work outpaced the growth in violent crime in general.

During the same period a series of publications based on the work of a variety of organizations and on research work were evidence themselves that violence at work was a source of concern. Employers' organizations, trade unions, professional bodies and others were all becoming increasingly aware of the problems of violence and the need to prevent them wherever possible and deal with them effectively when they occur. There is a general view that violence at work has been increasing. However, this is difficult to prove or disprove since there has not been large-scale systematic record keeping and there have been changes in the patterns of reporting incidents that could suggest an increase in incidents that may, in reality, be an increase in the reports of them as reporting becomes more acceptable.

The lack of data also makes it difficult to quantify either the levels of violence or any changes or differences year on year, geographically or in particular occupational groups. Despite their limitations the following pieces of work have contributed to a growing understanding of the nature, scale and effects of violence at work.

- In 1987 The Health and Safety Executive's Health Service Advisory Committee produced a report entitled 'Violence to Staff in the Health Services'. This report

15

suggested that violence to health service staff was far more common than previously believed. In some areas of work violence to staff was a regular occurrence. A survey of 3000 health service workers showed that in the previous year:

- 1 in 200 (0.5 per cent) had an injury requiring medical assistance;
- 11 per cent had a minor injury requiring first aid;
- 5 per cent had been threatened with a weapon;
- 18 per cent had been threatened verbally (see Figure 2.1).

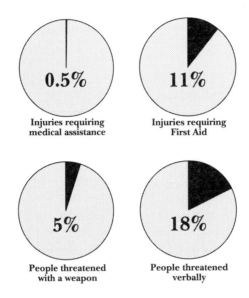

Figure 2.1 *Violence to staff in the health services*

- The TUC's report on 'Violence to Staff'* in 1988 highlighted the lack of a comprehensive body of data on violence at work and then reviewed current initiatives on violence to staff in a range of employment sectors and showed that awareness of the problem had increased but the nature and extent of the risks to employees was still unclear.

- The report of the DSS Advisory Committee on 'Violence to Staff' (1988) concluded that the issue should be considered in the wider context of service provision and against the legal background of the Health and Safety at Work Act 1974. The report made recommendations for all DSS services and argues that central strategies alone are insufficient; initiatives must take into account local circumstances. Where strategies for combating violence have not been developed the report proposed urgent action, even in certain services or areas where violence is not perceived as a problem.

    The report's principal recommendations are the development of local strategies which contain an assessment of the problem of violence, preventative measures, suitable responses, support of staff who are victims of violence and the importance of training in translating strategies into practical advice.

- The report of the Elton Committee 'Discipline in Schools',† considered the problems of violence and aggression. A survey of approximately 2500 teachers in secondary schools showed that in one week:

    - 15 per cent (1 in 7) had suffered verbal abuse;
    - 0.5 per cent (1 in 200) had experienced incidents involving actual violence (see Figure 2.2).

*TUC Report (1988), *Violence to Staff* Progress Report, Trades Union Congress.
†Elton Committee (1989), *Discipline in Schools*, Report of the Committee of Enquiry Chaired by Lord Elton. London: HMSO.

1 in 7 suffered
verbal abuse

1 in 200 experienced
violence

Figure 2.2   *Violence against teachers in one week*

- Department of Transport figures in 'Assaults on bus staff and measures to prevent such assaults' (April 1986) show that there were about 10 000 reported assaults on bus staff between 1979 and 1983.

- On London Buses Ltd there were 1350 assaults on bus drivers and conductors in 1985. Changes implemented in August 1986 resulted in a 20 per cent reduction in the number of assaults from January to September 1987 (*Personnel Management*, February 1988*)

- Within the DSS study figures show that:
  - 52 per cent of violent incidents occur in offices;
  - 40 per cent in the homes of claimants;
  - the remainder occur in the street, over the telephone and so on (see Figure 2.3).

  As only 20 per cent of the face-to-face contact with clients occurs in the claimant's home the figures indicate that a proportionately higher number of violent incidents take place during home visits (DSS Research Management Division, 1986).

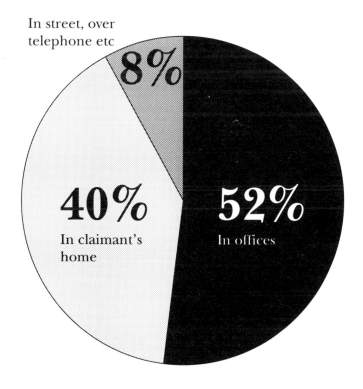

Figure 2.3   *Violence against DSS staff*

Personnel Management (February 1988), 'Protecting Employees from Attack'. Institute of Personnel Management.

- In 1988 The British Crime Survey* found that teachers, welfare workers and nurses are three times more likely than the average employee to be verbally abused or threatened. Other occupational groups with a similarly increased risk of abuse include managers in the entertainment sector, transport workers, male security guards and librarians.

- In 'The Risks in Going to Work' (Phillips, Stockdale and Joeman, 1989) research:

  - 8 per cent of people are likely to suffer an assault on their journey to or from work;

  - one in five are likely to experience an unpleasant incident on their journey;

  - one in five face threatening behaviour;

  - sexual harassment occurs most frequently with one in five victims being women in professional occupations where they spend a substantial amount of time away from a base, or workers in shops and offices;

  - the frequency of physical attacks ranges from a relatively low 4 per cent for female office workers to one in seven (approx. 15 per cent) for male professionals who often work away from the office;

  - the incidence of threatening behaviour varies from one in ten experiencing it among office-based professionals to one in three for those who often meet clients.

- The British Crime Survey for 1988 showed that 25 per cent of crime victims said that the incident had happened at, or because of, work. Fourteen per cent of respondents said they had been verbally abused at work at least once in the previous year and a third of all threats of violence were received at work.

*HMSO (1988), *British Crime Survey*, Home Office Research and Statistics Department.

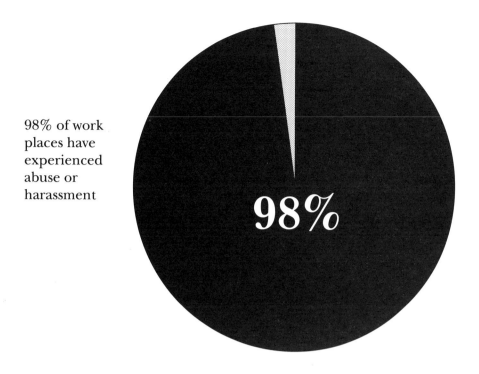

98% of work places have experienced abuse or harassment

Figure 2.4 *Violence against the public services*

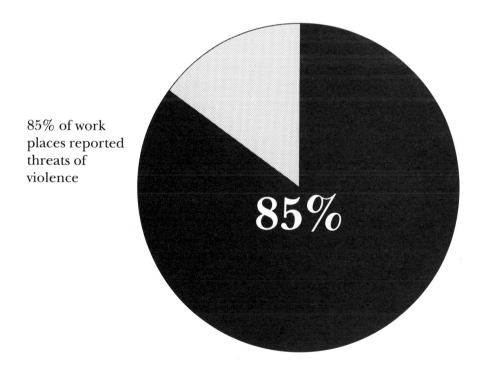

85% of work places reported threats of violence

Figure 2.5 *Violence against the public services*

- Research was published in 1987 by the Labour Research Department*. It was largely concerned with public services and showed that:

  - 98 per cent of workplaces had experienced instances of abuse or harassment (see page 19);
  - 85 per cent of workplaces reported that threats of violence had been made (see page 19);
  - 62 per cent of workplaces suffered one or more instances of actual violence, including 80 per cent of transport companies and 77 per cent of health authorities;
  - 28 per cent of workplaces had experienced violence using a weapon (see page 21).

In the survey of 210 workplaces with a total of over 86 000 employees more than two-thirds (67 per cent), felt that the level of abuse and violence had increased during the past five years (see Figures 2.4–2.8).

- The IDS Study 458 (May 1990) suggests that 'companies are not immune from the increase in violence in society in general' and goes on to cite the following examples:

  - Tesco reports hardly any attacks at all at the start of the 1980s, followed by an increase of 100 per cent per year for several years (Figure 2.9);
  - local authorities and hospitals report similar trends;
  - at Whitbread Inns, the rising incidence of violence prompted the Board to instigate a complete overhaul of training procedures in order to address the problem. Traditionally closing times and weekends were found to be particularly dangerous. Before the new training programme began to tackle the problems 50 per cent of violent incidents took place on Friday and Saturday nights and 50 per cent at closing time (see Figure 2.10).
  - transport and hospital staff in particular are especially at risk late at night and at weekends. Hospital casualty departments find that the vast majority of assaults on staff are clustered late on Friday and Saturday nights when they are busiest;
  - on London Underground about 30 per cent of all assaults on staff occur during the last three hours of operations, between 10 pm and 1 am (see Figure 2.11).

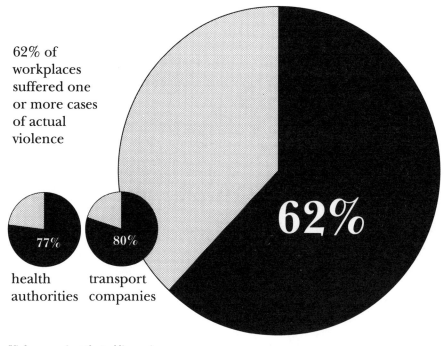

62% of workplaces suffered one or more cases of actual violence

77% health authorities

80% transport companies

62%

Figure 2.6 *Violence against the public services*

*Labour Research Department (July 1987), 'Assaults on Staff' *Bargaining Report* pp. 5–12.

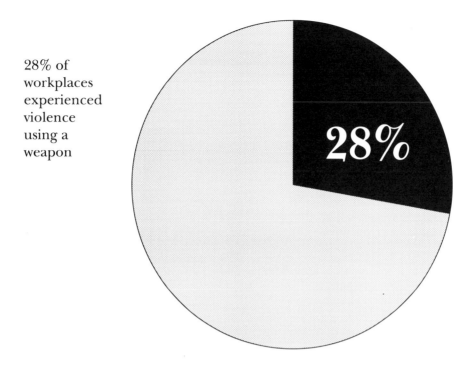

28% of
workplaces
experienced
violence
using a
weapon

Figure 2.7 *Violence against the public services*

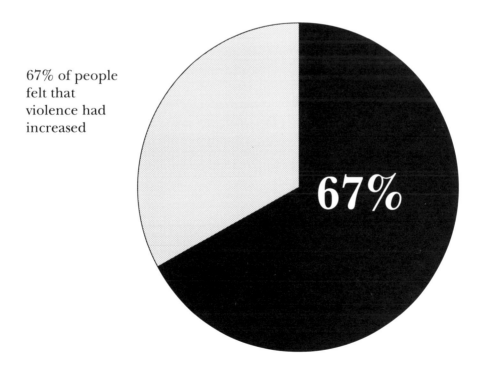

67% of people
felt that
violence had
increased

Figure 2.8 *Violence against the public services*

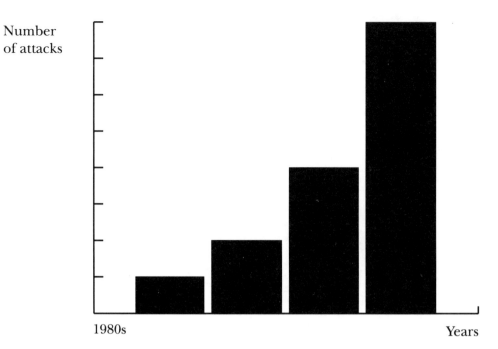

Number of attacks

1980s   Years

Figure 2.9 *Attacks on Tesco staff*

- The Which? Report* on Street Crime used the British Crime Survey (BCS) as its basis because of the belief that it was a better indicator of crime rates than police statistics. The BCS figures show that:
  - the likelihood of being mugged, even in a high-risk area, is less than the one in five chance of your car or something from it being stolen in a year;
  - mugging is more common in inner-city, multi-racial areas, council estates with low-income tenants and areas with 'non-family' housing (i.e. from bed-sits to large detached properties);
  - men are more at risk of crime overall than women and particularly of violent crime in the streets;
  - elderly people are less at risk from crime than young people and not simply because they go out less. It is young men who are most at risk of assault and robbery;
  - Afro-Caribbean and Asian people are more likely to be the victims of crime than white people;
  - Asian people are more likely to suffer vandalism, personal theft and victimization by groups of strangers (see Figure 2.12).

THE RISK OF CRIME

The fear of becoming a victim of crime, even violent crime, may be a 'healthy' fear based on knowledge that helps people protect themselves by making sensible, safe decisions. In some cases the fear can be very 'unhealthy' because it causes people great anxiety and severely limits the way they conduct their lives, both working and personal.

*Which? Report (November 1990), 'Street Crime', *Which? Magazine* pp. 636–39, Consumers' Association.

50% of violent incidents occurred on Friday and Saturday nights

50% of violent incidents occurred at closing time

Figure 2.10 *The timing of violent incidents*

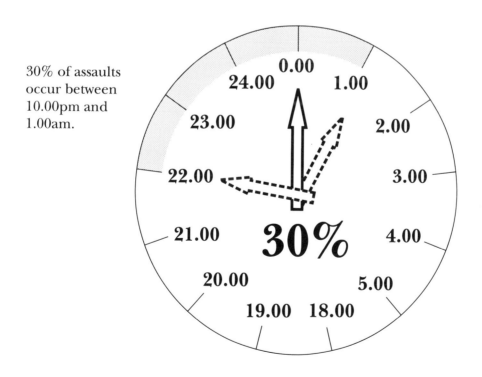

30% of assaults occur between 10.00pm and 1.00am.

Figure 2.11 *Assaults on London Underground staff*

23

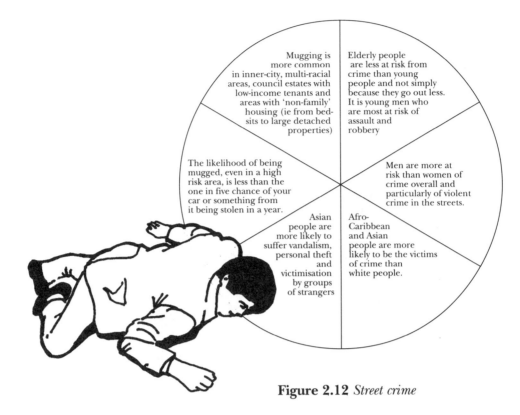

Figure 2.12 *Street crime*

Figure 2.12 *Street crime*

While fear of crime is understandable because of what we see and hear in the media or because of having been a victim or living in an area of high levels of crime, it is important to get the risks in perspective. In many cases the fear of crime is disproportionate to the actual risk.

A Home Office Study on 'Fear of Crime',* as well as other work, shows that the perceived level of crime sometimes bears little resemblance to the true level, especially crimes of violence and sexual offences. People very often overestimate the risk of becoming a victim, particularly of crimes of violence. Similarly, the proportion of all crimes that involve violence is generally overestimated.

The total number of notifiable offences recorded in the twelve months to the end of March 1991 was 4.7 million, a rise of 18 per cent over the previous twelve months. Of the 4.7 million crimes 94 per cent were crimes against property, 5 per cent (approximately 252 000) were crimes against the person and 1 per cent were other types of crimes (32 000) (see Figure 2.13).

There were over 250 000 more car crimes in the twelve months to March 1991, more than a third of the overall increase of 705 000 offences (see Figure 2.14).

There was a relatively small rise in violent crime of 4 per cent compared with rises of around 10 per cent in the previous three years (see Figure 2.15). These figures are derived from the notifiable offences recorded by the police in England and Wales in 1990–91; thus Scotland and Ireland are excluded as are any offences not notified or not recorded.

Taking the 1990–91 statistics, Figure 2.16 shows types of crime under the Home Office offence groups. Each type of crime is shown as a percentage of the total 4.7 million crimes with explanatory notes.

*Home Office Standing Committee for Violence (1984), *Report of the Working Group – Fear of Crime in England and Wales*, Home Office Public Relations Branch.

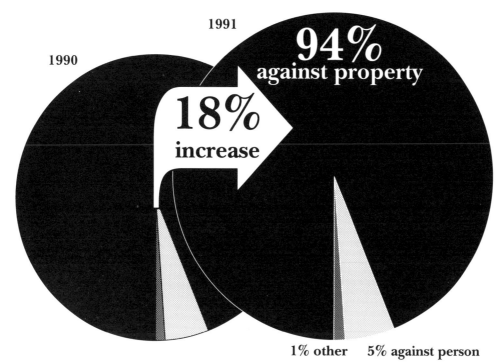

Figure 2.13 *The increase in crime*

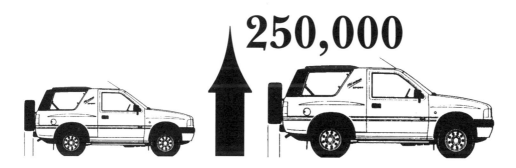

Figure 2.14 *Car crime*

Figure 2.14 *Increases in car crime*

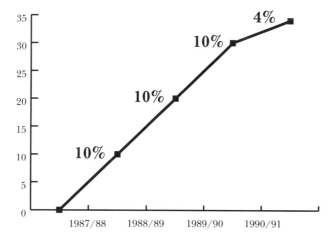

Figure 2.15 *The rise in violent crime*

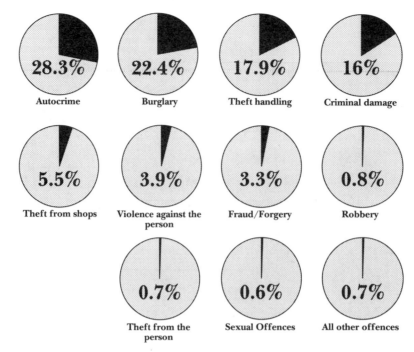

Figure 2.16 *Types of crime (expressed as a percentage of total number of crimes)*

Notes
Autocrime includes theft of property from a vehicle (17.2%) as well as theft of vehicles.
Burglary. About 20% of burglaries are effected without an entry being forced to premises. This figure includes burglaries in non-dwellings (10.7%) and in dwellings (11.7%)
Theft handling. This is theft of unattended property, handbags left on chairs, money in desk drawers, cheque books in coat pockets.
Criminal damage. Almost half of these crimes are against motor vehicles.
Theft from shops. This figure is largely made up of shoplifting offences.
Violence against the person. This category includes murder, attempted murder, manslaughter, assault, wounding and endangering life. The largest number of crimes under this heading are assaults and woundings.
Robbery is theft with violence, often called mugging, when an individual is robbed. This figure also includes robberies on banks, building societies and security vans.
Theft from the person. Also commonly called mugging, the forceful taking of property but not using violence against the person to carry out the crime.

It is clear from the figures that statistically crimes of violence against the person represent only a small proportion of all crimes. The chance of an individual being a victim of violent crime is far less than the chance they have of being a victim of auto crime.

However, it is important to remember that:

• even a small percentage of a total of 4.7 million crimes means there were 251 800 individual violent crimes in England and Wales in the year to March 1991;

• although a crime may not involve violence against the person within the legal definition it may still result in the victim feeling attacked and violated;

• many incidents of violence at work go unreported in the workplace, let alone to the police;

• the crime statistics can only indicate the statistical probability of being a victim of violent crime; they do not take account of individuals at greater risk because of the jobs they do or the lifestyle they lead;

• violent crime is not a gender issue in the way it is sometimes assumed to be, i.e. women are more at risk than men. In fact, many more victims of violent crime are men than women. The majority of assaults are by young men on young men.

Sexual offences

Sexual offences are often those that people, especially women, fear most and so warrant particular comment.

When we consider the range of sexual offences in detail it is clear that this category includes a number of offences as well as rape and indecent assault on women about which we so often hear in the media.

Sexual offences are recorded separately but they are nonetheless within the violent crime category.

In the year to March 1991 there were 29 044 sexual offences in England and Wales recorded by the police, 0.6 per cent of the total of all crimes. This figure represented a fall in the number of offences of 689 (or 2.3 per cent) over the previous year's recorded sexual offences.

The figures for the different types of crimes within the sexual offences category are shown as a percentage of the total of all sexual offences (see Figure 2.17).

Offence	*%*
Buggery	3.85
Indecent assault on a male	10.47
Indecency between males	3.9
Rape	11.67
Unlawful sexual intercourse	8.4
Indecent assault on a female	54.34
Incest	1.49
Procuration	0.6
Abduction	1.2
Bigamy	0.25
Gross indecency with a child	3.66

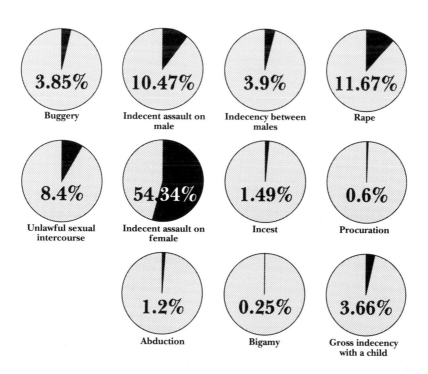

Figure 2.17   *Breakdown of sexual offences (expressed as a percentage of total of all sexual offences)*

As well as crime figures, other statistical information helps to put the risk of becoming a victim of a sexual offence into perspective. For example:

- about 40 per cent of rapes take place between people already known to each other;

- over 60 per cent of rapes take place in buildings, homes or offices, rather than in the dark alleys we hear of in the more sensational press (see Figure 2.18);

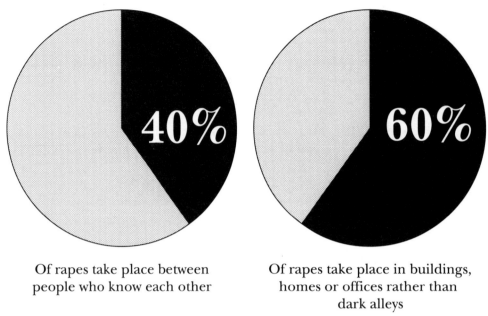

Of rapes take place between
people who know each other

Of rapes take place in buildings,
homes or offices rather than
dark alleys

Figure 2.18 *The statistics on rape*

- sexual offences against males are far more common than most people believe;

- you are more likely to become a rape victim between the ages of 16 and 24 and least likely under 10 years of age or over 60 (see Figure 2.19);

- the majority of convicted rapists are men in their twenties;

- contrary to popular belief about night-time risks, many assaults and attacks take place in the afternoon after pubs close and schools come out;

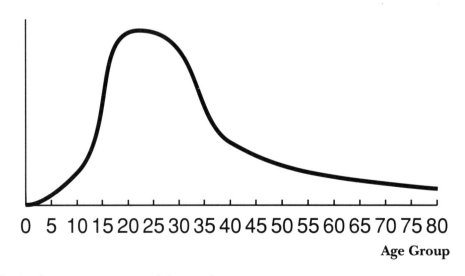

0 5 10 15 20 25 30 35 40 45 50 55 60 65 70 75 80

Age Group

Figure 2.19 *At what age are you most at risk from rape?*

28

- statistically any individual's chance of becoming a victim of a sexual offence is low, but other factors such as lifestyle, geographical location and occupation can change the probability.

Information of this sort can help in allaying unnecessary fears while enabling people to recognize real risks and thereafter make sensible judgements that will help to keep them safe. For example:

- women should not assume that they are safe because they are meeting a man they know through work, particularly if they will be on his premises;

- men should not assume they are safe from sexual offences simply because they are men;

- young women aged between 16 and 24 who are often in the company of men in their twenties and frequent pubs and clubs should be well advised to think about

  - whom they are with
  - whom they take home or go home with
  - who knows where they are
  - how they will travel home safely.

3
Employer and Employee Roles

The Health and Safety at Work Act, Section 2 (1) 1974* imposes a general obligation and specific applications of it upon employers. The general obligation is: 'it shall be the duty of every employer to ensure so far as is reasonably practicable, the health, safety and welfare of all his employees'. The matters to which that duty extends include:

- 'the provision and maintenance of plant and systems of work that are, so far as is reasonably practicable, safe and without risk to health';

- 'the provision of such information, instruction, training and supervision as is necessary to ensure, so far as is reasonably practicable, the health and safety at work of his employees';

- the provision and maintenance of a working environment for his employees that is, so far as is reasonably practicable, safe and without risk to health . . .'.

In addition there is an obligation to draw up and publish written safety policies to include these matters.

Apart from the obligations under the Health and Safety at Work Act, there are other obligations on an employer arising from:

- the employer's duty of care under Common Law for the safety of his employees;

- the employer's duty under any nationally negotiated agreements;

- the employer's duty not to dismiss employees unfairly. Employees have resigned in some situations and successfully alleged constructive unfair dismissal because the employer failed to provide reasonable precautions for the employee's safety, thus establishing a precedent.

Employers face penalties under the Health and Safety at Work Act if they fail to meet their obligations. Employees also have the option of seeking other remedies where any employer fails to fulfil his or her duty including damages, industrial action and resignation followed by a claim for constructive unfair dismissal.

The key question arising from this is 'what is meant by reasonably practicable?' The meaning is largely governed by case law of which the most important case is a Court of Appeal case, *Edwards* v *National Coal Board* (1949), IKB 704. In giving judgement Lord Justice Asquith said:

'reasonably practicable' is a narrower term than 'physically possible' and seems to me to imply that a computation must be made by the owner in which the quantum of

*Health and Safety Executive (1990), *A guide to The Health and Safety at Work etc. Act 1974*, 4th ed. London: HMSO.

risk is placed on one scale and the sacrifice involved in the measures necessary for averting the risk (whether in money, time or trouble) is placed in the other.

The principles of this case would apply to proceedings under the Health and Safety at Work Act or any other similar kind of proceedings. This means that:

- the burden of proof that all reasonably practicable measures have been taken rests upon the employer;

- the employers must be able to show that they had applied their minds to the computation mentioned by Lord Justice Asquith;

- courts will decide on the factual evidence whether the employers are entitled to rely upon the 'reasonably practicable' defence.

These principles have been upheld in a number of cases arising from areas of employment as varied as mining, local authorities and the entertainment industry. In other cases the judges have made it clear that there is a requirement on employers to:

- take action to minimize risks to employees;

- take into account the risk of criminal attack as part of the obligation to provide a safe system of work.

The enforcement of The Health and Safety at Work Act can be

- by an improvement notice, when an inspector considers health and safety legislation is being contravened;

- by a prohibition notice when an inspector considers there is a risk of serious personal injury;

- by prosecution for breach of The Health and Safety at Work Act or its relevant statutory provisions.

A breach of Sections 2–6 of The Health and Safety at Work Act attracts a £20 000 fine; breach of other relevant statutory provisions £2000 (£5000 from October 1992). Magistrates may imprison for up to six months individuals who fail to comply with an improvement or prohibition notice; in the Crown Court the period is two years.

Another aspect of The Health and Safety at Work Act is sometimes forgotten, that is the duty it places upon individuals. In S7 of The Act it is made clear that it is the 'duty of every employee to take reasonable care for the health and safety of himself and other people who may be affected by his act or omissions at work'.

Of particular interest is S37 which shows that offences under the Act may be committed either by individual people or by corporate bodies such as limited companies, nationalized industries or local authorities. If an offence committed by a corporate body was committed with the consent or connivance of or because of the negligence of a director, manager, secretary or other officer, that party is also guilty of the offence, and may be prosecuted as well as the corporate body.

Although prosecutions of individuals under this provision have been rare it is well worth managers and others remembering its existence and the implications for them personally.

The balance struck within the Act between employer and employee responsibility is extremely important. It is pointless for an employer to develop safe working practices if members of the workforce do not observe the rules of safe working, fail to follow the procedures laid down or otherwise put themselves and/or others at risk, for example through practical jokes or horseplay resulting in injury. Similarly an employee can strive to work safely but his/her ability to do so can be severely limited without the commitment and support of the employer.

It is not only the statutory responsibility or other imposed obligations that provide the motivation to develop safe working practices. There are personal and organizational costs associated with violence in the workplace. Personal attack or injury can lead to:

- time off work as a result of an injury itself or psychological damage caused by it that leads to depression, insomnia, agoraphobia or panic attacks;

- litigation against the employer;

- compensation claims;

- higher insurance costs;

- bad publicity for the organization;

- loss of confidence;

- anxiety and stress;

- fear of certain aspects of jobs or jobs themselves.

Any form of violence, whether or not it results in some sort of physical injury, can have serious adverse effects on the workforce, including:

- high levels of anxiety;

- stress-related illness;

- absenteeism and the need to cover for staff;

- low morale;

- high levels of staff turnover;

- low productivity;

- little job satisfaction;

- low employee involvement;

- industrial action or poor industrial relations;

- difficulty in recruiting and retaining staff.

In companies where there is an endemic problem of violence there is a tendency to accept it as part of the job. This is a dangerous tendency, both in the sense that it ignores a problem with potentially very serious consequences for individuals and the organization, and also because the tendency to dismiss the problem frequently comes from managers or others who are least likely to suffer directly from the problem.

Despite the clear duties and obligations placed on employers and employees there are many workplaces with very limited arrangements for tackling the problem of violence at work, some workplaces have no arrangements at all.

The Labour Research Department *Bargaining Report** found that:

- less than half the workplaces where actual violence had occurred (45 per cent) had any system of monitoring violent incidents;

- more than two-thirds (67 per cent) felt that the level of violence/abuse had increased in recent years;

- less than one-third of workplaces (31 per cent) had a management structure providing someone with overall responsiblity for dealing with abuse/violence;

- 86 per cent of workplaces felt that their management should take more responsiblity for the health and safety of staff exposed to risks of abuse/violence;

*Labour Research Department (July 1987), 'Assaults on Staff' *Bargaining Report* pp. 5–12.

- despite the fact that 62 per cent of the workplaces surveyed had experienced actual violence, only 11 per cent had taken industrial action over the issue (see Figure 3.1).

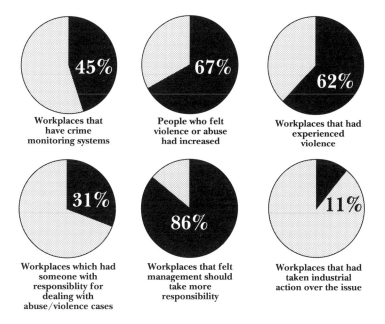

Figure 3.1 *Personal safety in the workplace*

The Health and Safety Executive's booklet *Violence to Staff* suggests that the best way to tackle violence in the workplace is for employers and employees to work together through an action plan.

The proposed action plan has the following seven steps with the key points in each step identified.

Step 1.   Find out if there is a problem

- It is easy for employers to think there is not a problem; employees may feel differently.

- The easiest way to find out about problems is by asking staff either informally or by using a formal method such as a questionnaire.

- Communicate the result of any investigation to staff. If there is a problem they then know the employer recognizes it; if there is not a problem any unfounded fears will be put to rest.

- If a survey does not identify a problem things could still change, so it is wise to check the situation from time to time.

Step 2.   Record all incidents

- Keeping records helps build up a picture of the problem. A simple form can be used to gather the details needed, e.g. what happened, when, where and to whom.

- Employees may not be keen to report incidents if they accept violence as part of the job or feel reporting it will reflect badly on them; having a reporting system and communicating the fact that reports are needed to tackle the problem can encourage reporting.

Step 3.   Classify all incidents

- The reporting system should classify all incidents so that details about the location, frequency, severity, nature and consequences of the incident can be gathered.

33

- Classification can assist in identifying areas or types of work where particular problems occur, patterns of incidents and, in some cases, causes and so help target any steps taken to tackle the problems.

- The classification used will depend on needs. It is easy to classify fatal injury, major injury, physical injury requiring hospital treatment or first aid and injury requiring time off work. It is less easy to classify incidents where the result is emotional shock, feelings of threat or effects requiring counselling or time off work.

- Any classification should be understood by all those using it and used consistently.

Step 4.   Search for preventive measures

- Finding appropriate preventive measures rarely means selecting off-the-shelf solutions to problems. The key is being clear about what the problem is and then devising ways of overcoming it that will work in particular circumstances.

- Employees who perform the jobs where there are risks can be a good source of ideas, as can other similar organizations with procedures in place, health and safety specialists, the police or security advisers.

- It is important that both employers and employees are open to solutions that require changes in procedures and working practices. Sometimes solutions may be perceived as less efficient but in the long term prove to be cost-effective.

Step 5.   Decide what to do

- Employees are more likely to be committed to any measures that they help to design and put into practice. Often trade union representatives and health and safety officers have experience in measures that can be taken.

- A mix of measures can often work best by balancing the risks to employees with any possible side effects of measures on the public, clients or customers that could increase the potential for violence.

Step 6.   Put measures into practice

- Whatever measures are decided on, the policy for dealing with violence should be included in the health and safety policy statement so that all employees are aware of it. This will encourage cooperation in following procedures and reporting incidents.

Step 7.   Check that measures work

- Once the preventive measures have been in place for a time it is important to check how well they are working.

- There are various methods to help with assessment such as comparing the number and types of incidents, the level of reporting of incidents and changes in employees' feelings about the situation.

- Often joint management and trade union committees are an effective means of jointly monitoring the measures.

- If the measures work, keep them up.

- If the measures are not effective, reassessing the problems and finding alternative measures may be necessary.

Of course these steps can be embodied in a policy – this is dealt with in Chapter 5.

4
Identifying Risks at Work

Once it has been recognized that employers and employees both have a duty in respect of safe working practices, and that not combating violence at work has potentially serious costs, many organizations start to take positive steps to tackle the problems.

The first step has to be that of identifying the risks. Some types of work have very obvious risks of violence associated with them, for example, jobs involving a great deal of direct contact with the public, a large amount of travelling, unsocial hours or handling money. However, this should not lead anyone to assume that there are jobs without any risks. Almost all jobs require people to get to and from a place of work and there are risks associated with travelling; the premises in which most people work could be susceptible to a break-in and almost no one works in such isolation that there is no risk from contacts they have – or even colleagues.

There are, of course, certain jobs recognized as having a relatively higher risk of violence attached to them. The Health and Safety Executive breaks down these jobs into the following categories:

Giving a service	benefits office, housing department
Caring	nurses, social workers, community care staff
Education	teachers, non-teaching staff
Money transactions	post offices, banks, shops, building societies, bus drivers/ conductors
Delivery/collection	milk delivery, postal services, rent collection
Controlling	reception staff, security staff, traffic wardens
Inspecting	environmental health officers, trading standards officers, building inspectors, planning officers

Within each of the Health and Safety Executive's categories are just a few examples of jobs that may fall into them. While most jobs could fit into one or other of these categories it would be possible to go on creating other categories too, for example:

Entertainment	pubs, clubs, concert or dance halls, sports grounds
Retailing	department stores, off-licences, late night shops, garages

Just because a particular type of business or organization is not on the list it cannot be assumed to be safe; it is still well worth investigating the potential risks of violence to staff.

One way of finding out if there is a problem and identifying the risks at work is to conduct an audit – a detailed, systematic, official investigation. An audit would look at what is done but also at how things are done as this is very often where the problems lie. The fact that

35

an audit is, by definition, an 'official' investigation is important because it implies organizational commitment to the exercise and an intention to act upon its findings.

If there is no intention or commitment to act on any findings of an audit it may be as well to not undertake one. An audit could raise both awareness and expectations among employees and a lack of action on the employer's part could lead to quite serious problems.

To conduct an audit it is necessary to decide where to investigate and the methods that will be used to obtain the information required.

WHERE TO INVESTIGATE

Trying to investigate an organization as a whole may be an impossible task, especially if it is large, has a number of different sites or sections or departments doing different types of work.

Investigating site by site or departments separately can make the task much more manageable. It helps to identify site- or department-specific issues, or problems associated with particular types of activity. The common issues can of course be identified and dealt with as such.

Whether an investigation considers the whole organization or a part at a time it ought to look at the workplace itself as well as the activities undertaken and the patterns of work. The following list suggests some areas worth investigation and poses some questions that an investigation or audit should seek to answer. The list is obviously not exhaustive and should be added to to reflect the organizational circumstances.

Access

- How is access to the building or buildings controlled?

- Are main entrances, side entrances, fire doors, loading bays, delivery areas and other access points subject to controls of any kind?

- Who knows who is in the building/s?

- Is there any way of identifying legitimate visitors?

- Could people just wander in? Do they?

- Do staff who control access have any means of summoning help or escaping?

- Is there a procedure for removing people from the building/s if necessary?

- Have there been problems with people coming into the workplace? If so, who? How did they get in? What happened?

Isolation

- Are employees working in isolated offices or parts of the building/s alone?

36

- Do employees conduct meetings with people or interview members of the public in isolated offices?

- Who knows where employees are and whom they are with?

- Can employees in isolated areas summon help or raise an alarm?

- Can anyone see or go to check on an employee alone with a client or customer?

- Have there been problems arising from employees working in isolation? If so, what happened? Is the problem happening often? Are there any procedures in the event of any employee getting into difficulty?

- Do staff feel fearful of isolation?

Reception

- Is there a reception area?

- Is the receptionist vulnerable or protected by a counter, screen or other means?

- Do reception staff have notice of who is expected?

- Is there a check-in procedure or record of visitors?

- Do the receptionists issue passes?

- Can they raise an alarm or escape to safety if necessary?

- Are receptionists expected to prevent people getting in or getting past them? Can they do so safely?

- Is there a procedure for dealing with unexpected visitors?

- What happens about contractors, deliveries, maintenance services etc?

- Have there been any incidents of violence in the reception area? If so, what happened? How and why do people think it happened?

Collecting money

- Who collects money?

- Are people collecting money protected from other people by screens, counters, till guards or other devices?

- How is money kept? In a till, locking drawer, a safe? Is the system adequate?

- Are alarms available to people collecting money? Are they obvious to an attacker or can the alarm be raised unobtrusively?

- How often are tills or cash drawers cleared?

- Are there any security cameras or other devices? Are they used properly?

- Are signs clearly displayed warning potential attackers of security systems?

- Are staff aware of and able to operate security procedures?

- Do staff feel safe collecting money? If not, why not?

Moving money

- Is money paid into or collected from banks or elsewhere regularly? Does this happen on the same day each week or at the same time?

- Who moves money?

- Are employees ever expected to move money without an escort? What security back-up is there when money is carried?

- Who knows about the movements of money?

- Do staff feel safe or threatened when involved in the movement of money? What are their particular concerns?

- Have there been any incidents involving staff moving money? If so, what happened?

- Are staff provided with personal attack alarms or other devices such as two way radios when moving money?

- What is the procedure in the event of an attack? Are staff aware of it and able to operate it?

- Are there safer ways of moving money?

Night working, late working, overtime working

- Are employees expected to work late, at night or do overtime? Is it regular or infrequent, unplanned or planned?

- What facilities are there for people to get home safely?

- Are taxis, mini-buses or other services provided?

- Are car parks and other areas safe at night?

- Could overtime or additional hours be done in the daytime at weekends instead of at night?

- Do people feel safe working late or at night and travelling home afterwards?

- Have there been incidents of violence associated with these patterns of working? If so, what happened? When?

- What security procedures operate after normal working hours?

Other people's premises/homes

- Are staff required to work in other people's premises or homes? Are they likely to be welcome or unwelcome?

- What records are kept and by whom of where staff are, whom they are with, how long they should be, when they are expected back?

- Are contact names and numbers kept for staff working away from the base?

- Are people requesting meetings or visits checked out before staff go to see them on their premises or in their homes?

- Is there a procedure for staff calling in if they feel at risk, change their plans or are delayed?

- What happens if staff cannot be contacted or do not return when expected? Who is responsible for taking action?

- Are diaries left in the office with client names, appointment times, location of meetings etc?

- Can people work in pairs if they feel at risk or refuse to go to an appointment?

- Are staff provided with personal alarms, two-way radios, mobile telephones?

- Do staff feel at risk when they are working away from their base? If so, why? What would alleviate their concerns?

- What procedures exist for staff working in others' premises or homes? Are staff aware of them and are they used?

- Have there been incidents of violence to staff? If so, where, when, who was involved, what happened?

Travel

- Are employees required to travel in the course of their work?

- What means of travel do employees use?

- Who knows the details of their journeys, visits, meetings, return times etc.?

- How is contact maintained between employees and their base?

- Does the organization provide vehicle breakdown service, car 'phones, mobile 'phones, personal alarms?

- Are there procedures for safe travel, safe parking, what to do in the event of a vehicle breakdown, action if stranded somewhere? Are employees aware of the procedures and how to use them?

- Have employees experienced incidents of violence when travelling? If so, what happened, when, where?

Workplace, location/environs

- Is the workplace itself isolated?

- Does it have controlled entry systems?

- Are employees expected to receive visitors in isolated locations?

- Do any employees work alone in isolated locations? What particular steps are taken to ensure their safety?

- Is the workplace well lit so people can be seen and see in the grounds, stairways, car parks etc.?

- Are there obstacles to good visibility around the workplace such as bushes or fences?

- Have there been incidents of violence around the workplace or in isolated locations? What happened, where, when?

Customers, clients and other people

- Who is likely to come to the organization, or receive a service from it?

- Are people likely to come to complain?

- Does the organization deal with people who are likely to be concerned, upset, annoyed, worried, angry?

- Are employees likely to have to deal with people with a high potential for violence, e.g. people who are drunk, on drugs?

- Are people kept waiting or dealt with promptly?

- Do staff feel under threat or fearful because of the people they have to deal with?

- What procedures exist to deal with situations where people become violent? Do staff know of them?

- Are the tasks the employees have to perform likely to bring them into conflict with other people, e.g. enforcement, inspection?

INVESTIGATION METHODS

When selecting investigation methods it is wise to pause before making a choice to answer some basic questions. This process will help in identifying an effective, acceptable and manageable method that will suit the particular circumstances.

What information do you want?

- Do you want information about the whole organization; one or more departments, or sections; groups of staff thought to be at risk or employees who undertake particular jobs or tasks?

- Do you want to collect information about people's feelings and attitudes to the problem of violence at work; identify gaps in safety measures; test out the level of awareness of staff in relation to safety procedures or collect data on actual incidents of violence?

What form of information do you want?

- Some methods generate so-called 'hard data', yes/no answers, numerical scores, choices from a list, ticks on a chart etc. These are data that can be quantified readily and information such as percentages derived from them.

- Other methods generate information which is much more difficult to quantify: views, opinions and anecdotal evidence are potentially infinitely variable because you do not put limits on the choice of responses to the questions and everyone will answer in their own way.

- Do you want numerical information such as the number of incidents of violence, the percentage of people that feel at risk or rankings of what employees believe are the most dangerous tasks?

- Do you want information in the form of descriptions of procedures used, anecdotal evidence of people's experiences of violent incidents or near misses, or, perhaps individual views about what are unsafe practices and how they could be improved?

- The simpler the information you collect the easier it will be to use. How simple can you keep your investigation but still get the information you need?

How much information should you collect?

- There is often a tendency to collect as much information as possible in one process. However, how much of each type of information can you handle effectively? Will you have any help when it comes to analysing it? How experienced are you and others in analysing and presenting information? Collecting information you cannot use is a waste of time.

- What levels of commitment and resources are there in the organization? Collecting more information than can be acted upon because of lack of commitment or re-sources is also a waste of time. It may also raise expectations that cannot be fulfilled and thus create problems.

- What timescales are you working to and what can realistically be achieved in that time?

Who should conduct the investigation?

- Who has skills or experience in information collection and management? Is external help a good idea and/or possible?

- If management conducts the investigation will staff feel able to be open and honest, critical if necessary or willing to admit a lack of understanding or confidence? Will the outcomes be accepted as reliable by everyone?

- If staff representatives investigate will management feel able to accept the findings without reservation?

- Could an existing, or created, joint management and staff group be responsible for conducting the investigation? This is often regarded as the best option to secure contributions, cooperation and commitment to the process and its outcomes.

An investigation does not have to be a complex or long-winded process; frequently the simple, straightforward approach generates information that can be readily analysed and acted upon. Like most things, the preparation for an investigation makes subsequent conduct and use of the information gathered very much easier. It is well worth making time at the planning stage to do the groundwork thoroughly as this will increase the chances of getting exactly what you need from the investigation, in a form that is manageable and will actually save time in the long run.

A few examples of methods of collecting information with some guidelines on using them and points about them follow.

Questionnaires

- Decide who is responsible for the investigation.

- Be quite clear about what information you want to collect so that the questionnaire can be constructed to do this.

- Keep it as simple as possible.

- Agree who will be involved in the construction, application and analysis of the questionnaire and their roles

- Only collect information you can handle and use.

- Questionnaires can be a useful method of collecting information from a large number of people.

- The response rate to questionnaires can be very low unless people are committed to contributing to the process through understanding its purpose.

- Questionnaires with closed questions or structured to elicit yes/no responses, ticks in boxes, a choice from limited options or a score on a scale produce data that can be readily quantified and are fairly easy to manage.

- Questionnaires with open questions asking for views, opinions, suggestions or descriptions generate much more anecdotal information or unique responses that can be difficult to analyse, collate and/or draw conclusions from.

- Consider whether or not the questionnaire can be anonymous. People may feel more able to be open and honest if it is; on the other hand you may need to be able to identify them, their department, the type of job and so on in order to be able to act on any findings.

- Some assurance about the confidentiality of replies to questionnaires and how this will work can help encourage people to reply and to do so openly.

- Not everyone will have the same level of literacy skills so the language and construction of the questionnaire may need to take this into account.

- The more targeted a questionnaire is (e.g. to specific groups of staff, people doing particular jobs, a section of a department) the more specific the questions can be and the more closely particular aspects of a situation can be investigated.

- A questionnaire can be a relatively simple means of collecting information quickly from a large number of people; on the other hand if it is badly prepared it is likely to be confusing, generate random data that cannot be managed or fail to provide the information it was intended to collect. If in any doubt about developing a questionnaire it is wise to get specialist help.

- If people are being asked to put time and effort into completing a questionnaire they will want to know the outcome as quickly as possible. Schedule the process of collecting, collating, analysing and producing findings, and agree when, how and to whom the findings will be communicated.

Observation

- Observing people at work and the process and procedures they operate can be an effective way of spotting risks or hazards that people doing the jobs are so familiar with that they may not recognize them.

- Decide what information you want.

- Agree who will undertake the observation, e.g. managers, supervisors, a joint management/staff team, consultants.

- A brief needs to be prepared for observers explaining what to look for and how to record findings.

- Recording findings has to be consistent if the information provided is to be comparable from all the observers and manageable.

- People may be inhibited by being observed or may do things in a way they do not normally do them; an observer can influence simply by being there.

- Observation can be time-consuming and/or costly if a reasonable cross section of people or jobs is to be observed in order to provide reliable data.

- Staff being observed need to be clear about the purpose of the observation: what information will be used, how and by whom; how confidentiality will apply and so on. Otherwise they may not feel able to cooperate.

- Decide in what form and to whom observers will report their findings at the outset so the task can be appropriately organized.

- Agree how the findings will be communicated generally.

- If outside consultants undertake the observation they can bring a degree of objectivity that people familiar with the organization and its operation may not have.

- Consultants may be more acceptable as observers to staff and management if they are perceived as being independent, having specialist expertise and are working to a jointly agreed brief.

- Deciding (jointly) to use outside observers without the knowledge of staff is also an option. This has certain obvious advantages but raises many issues about openness and involvement.

Structured interviews

- Structured interviews, done well, can provide the best of both worlds: one-to-one interaction with control of the information generated by using agreed questions and recording systems throughout.

43

- As with all methods it is important to be clear about the information required and in what form.

- Structured interview questions can be 'closed', requiring the interviewer to tick choices, circle responses or underline from a list. Questions can also be 'open' where the interviewer's task is more complex. In this case a recording process that picks out key points, facts, feelings, views or other information relative to the question is helpful. Keeping even 'open' questions limited in scope and specific makes recording easier.

- Interviewing people is a good way of getting them to 'open up' about problems, risks they perceive, their fears and concerns, experiences they have had or obtaining detailed information about practice.

- Interviewing can be very time-consuming if done well.

- Structured interviewing, because it is built around previously agreed questions and recording processes, can become mechanistic if the interviewers are not skilled.

- A carefully designed recording process is as important as carefully designed questions if it is to produce consistent, accurate and manageable data from all the interviews.

- Structured questions and recording processes help to ensure the objectivity of the interviewers.

- Decide who will do the interviewing. The interviewers need to be skilled, or to be trained, and they need to be acceptable to the interviewees as well as people who will use the information and the findings they generate.

- Jointly agreeing and/or developing and designing the structured interviews with employee representatives can help ensure cooperation and the acceptability of the results.

- Employees should be informed about the structured interview process, its purpose and their role in contributing to it.

- Interviewers and interviewees need to be clear about how and to whom information gathered will be passed and how any agreements on confidentiality will be managed.

- Recording of interviews using cassette tapes is a possibility. However, this may inhibit people and they will still have to be listened to again in order to transfer responses to a recording system for analysis.

- Structured interviews with groups is a means of gathering a range of views at one time but they are difficult to manage and require a very skilled interviewer and/or very sophisticated recording techniques.

- Time invested in the planning and design of structured interviews is essential if the reward is to be useful and usable information.

- If the expertise to develop a structured interview process is not available in the organization you should consider obtaining outside help or employing consultants with the appropriate expertise.

Working groups

- Group approaches to identifying possible risks or hazards can work very well because managers, staff representatives, people working in particular areas or jobs, safety officers and so on can all be involved and bring their different perspectives to bear. However, if the group is too big it will be unmanageable.

- A working group will need clear terms of reference, clearly defined tasks, roles and power, resources to do the job and a timetable.

- The group will need to be clear about what is expected from it as a final product, in what form, for whom and how it will be used in order to organize their tasks appropriately.

- It is important to be clear from the start what the status of the findings of the group will be.

- As with any working group there is a risk that it may become a 'talking shop' or develop a life of its own! Avoid this by putting time and effort into setting it up properly with finite tasks and an agreed lifetime wherever possible.

- Information about the working group should be communicated to employees to ensure they know what is going on, why, how the group will work and their role in contributing to the work of the group.

- Working groups can employ a range of methods in their investigation; they will need to be clear about how the information generated in different ways will be brought together.

- The variety of members in a working group can be helpful in that different members may be more or less acceptable to different employees because of their skills, experience, being known by the people or their representative roles. Thus tasks can be allocated to the most appropriate person to get the best possible results.

- A working group that is representative may be more generally acceptable as everyone can feel their views are being fed into the process. In addition the findings of a representative group may be generally 'owned', or more so than those of differently constituted groups.

- The working group will need to gain the confidence of employees so they need to be able to explain their role and task, how the outcomes will be used and how issues such as confidentiality will be managed.

- Communicating the findings of the group needs to be planned as part of their task, including communicating generally with employees.

Consultants

- Identifying consultants to undertake an investigation on your behalf can be helpful as you can select people with the particular skills you require, e.g. experts in safety matters, specialist researchers.

- Using consultants can be a speedy and cost-effective way of working if properly managed because they can devote time and attention to the process that few employees have; thus the cost may be less than using employees.

- When choosing a consultant you need to be sure you have the right person or persons for the job:
  - check their track record and experience;
  - make sure the approach they will use is acceptable;

45

- ensure they can meet your timescale;
- check that you can provide the support and resources needed;
- confirm that it is a cost-effective option;
- ensure their style is appropriate for your organization.

- You must brief consultants properly and fully, i.e. you must be clear about what you are trying to achieve. The brief should cover:

  - what you expect them to achieve, be precise about the task, problem, needs etc;
  - terms of reference;
  - the outcomes you require and in what form;
  - what you want to do with the outcomes;
  - timescale they are to meet;
  - what you or others will do to support or assist them;
  - who will manage their work, to whom they report, when and how;
  - what resources are available to them;
  - how you expect them to work and with whom;
  - how issues such as confidentiality will be dealt with.

  Clearly a formal contract is preferable when working with consultants so much of the briefing information can be included in that.

- It is essential to communicate to employees about the consultants, their task and role. Otherwise they may be perceived as 'management spies' and people may not feel they can cooperate fully.

- It may be worthwhile agreeing on the task and the consultant/s in a joint forum with employees or their representatives. In this way the consultant/s can work on behalf of the joint group.

- Beware of 'dumping' the responsiblity for the investigation on consultants. Consultants should work with you if the investigation is to be effective, not take over and do the job for you.

- Remember that the problems and issues identified by the consultants are the responsibility of the organization and you will need to agree how you will act upon the findings of the consultants.

- You will need to agree a way of communicating the consultants' findings to employees, particularly where they have contributed to the investigation.

OTHER METHODS

Apart from the methods dealt with here, there are other ways of investigating risks at work, all of which have advantages and disadvantages, for example:

- suggestion boxes;
- through team meetings with supervisors or managers;
- staff meetings or departmental meetings;
- asking people to write in with views, ideas, problems, opinions etc;

46

- open forum meetings with, e.g. safety, welfare or personnel staff;

- going to visit other workplaces to observe different practices in operation.

When selecting a method ensure that it will meet your needs, will be manageable, that you can resource it properly, it fits into your timescale and it will produce information that can be acted upon.

No method is perfect, or capable of giving you exactly what you want every time. A complex method is not necessarily the most effective method; simple methods that can be used easily and quickly are sometimes the best approach.

Whatever method you choose do make sure people know what is being done and why, involve them whenever possible and let them know the outcome as quickly as you can.

Finally, act upon the findings as soon as is practicable. You may discover risks or hazards that can be dealt with immediately, tackle them straightaway, thus reassuring people of the commitment to act. Other more complex problems may take time to deal with. In this situation it is important to keep people in touch with the progress that is being made so that they know the problem is being tackled. This also helps to maintain confidence.

5
Developing Policy and Procedures

The Health and Safety at Work Act places certain obligations on employers and employees in respect of safety at work. Probably the best way of translating those obligations into responsibilities and actions to be taken is by developing a formal, written policy.

In this sense a policy is a document that sets out the course of action to be pursued by the organization (employers and employees) in order to fulfil its obligations in law and in respect of national or workplace agreements.

A policy provides a framework on which procedures and practices can be built. It makes it possible to require or demand appropriate behaviour or action in relation to safety matters. Furthermore, a policy provides clarity, demonstrates commitment and develops confidence in the organization's willingness to address the issue of violence at work. While the responsibility for policy is a managerial one the usual, and generally most effective, process for developing policy is a joint one where management and staff negotiate and agree it.

Developing any policy, especially where meeting its requirements can have a cost to the organization (in financial, resource or time terms) or to the individual (in terms of demands on them, required behaviour, changes in practice) can be fraught with difficulty. The management and staff roles in negotiating it can become adversarial and time-consuming. The consultative mechanisms can be extremely protracted. Worst of all, it can end up so watered down in becoming acceptable that it does not achieve its purpose.

Having said all that, a policy that is not jointly developed, negotiated and agreed is unlikely to be 'owned' by people generally so may not have their commitment or confidence. Before starting the process of developing the policy it is helpful to be clear about a number of points:

- Who needs to be involved in the development process and how? Management, staff representatives, Board members, specialist staff? What are their powers and remit?

- Who needs to be a party to agreements? Board members, managers with delegated authority, trade union representatives, representatives of non-union staff?

- The timescale for the development, consultation process and agreement to the policy.

- The resources and support that will be required throughout the process.

- The limited availability of busy people can slow the process considerably. Being clear about the priority given to this task and planning meeting dates helps to keep to the timescale.

- The tasks may not be straightforward or easy and people who commit themselves to assisting in the process should understand what their commitment entails.

- The policy may mean changes or costs that people will wish to resist. Management and the development group need to be very clear about the extent to which they must take views into account and the extent to which they may impose their own.

THE POLICY DOCUMENT

The following list identifies areas that would normally be covered by a policy on violence at work.

1. **Policy title**. The policy title needs to make it clear what the policy is about in general terms. Examples of titles include: 'Combating Violence at Work'; 'XYZ Ltd Policy on Violence to Staff'; 'Safety from Violence at Work – a Policy Statement'; 'Health and Safety Policy – Violence to Staff'.

   If the policy on violence to staff is part of an overall health and safety policy it ought to be identifiable within the main policy and an obvious title can help.

2. **The purpose** (or aim or objective). This should be a general statement of what the policy is intended to achieve. It does not need to go into any detail. For example the purpose could be described as follows:

   - To prevent the risks to staff from violence.

   - To fulfil legal and other obligations by ensuring the safety of staff.

   - To protect staff from all forms of violence whenever possible and provide aftercare should staff fall victim to violence.

   - To ensure that everyone in the organization is aware of and fulfils their responsiblity for safety from violence at work.

3. **Definition** – what the organization and this particular policy means by violence at work. What behaviour and actions are included and excluded from the definition of violence used (see also Chapter 1).

4. **The philosophy**. This section describes the basis from which the policy starts, the values and beliefs underlying it that can be expressed as a series of statements, for example:

   - All violence to staff is unacceptable, whatever form it takes and whatever reasons are cited for it.

   - We recognize the risks to staff from violence at work and the obligations of the organization to minimize the risks.

   - Dealing with, or being subject to, violent behaviour is not considered to be a failure on the part of an employee.

   - Violence is not considered to be an acceptable part of any job nor is it part of the duties of any employee to accept violent behaviour.

49

- We recognize the potentially damaging effects of violence on individuals, work performance and the organization as a whole and are committed to combating it.

5. **Whom the policy covers**. All staff in the organization may be subject to the policy and its requirements or it may be a policy developed for a particular site, department or group of staff with a unique role in the organization.

   It is also important to be clear about whether the policy applies to permanent staff only or to contracted staff, temporary staff, consultants or others who may be working in the organization for a short time.

6. **What the employer is committed to do**. Examples of the actions that the employer will take include:

   - Analysis/audit within the organization to identify risks, hazards, problems or other issues.

   - Preventative measures to combat the risks of violence at work such as changes in the environment, procedures and practices.

   - Data collection or monitoring of incidents of violence to staff and actions as a result of the information gathered.

   - Communication of the policy to ensure that everyone is aware of it and their responsibility in respect of it.

   - Allocation of specific roles and responsibilities in support of the policy such as: assigning a manager with overall responsibility for the policy; responsibility for monitoring incidents; responsibility for ensuring appropriate aftercare for victims; responsibility for safety training.

   - Sanctions to be taken in the event of violent behaviour by an employee of the organization.

   - Aftercare procedures to be made available such as: counselling; time off work; earnings protection; help in bringing a court case; assistance with compensation claims or medical assistance.

   - Evaluation and review of the policy and procedures at agreed intervals and the continual development of practice.

   - Putting in place of an appropriate joint management and staff forum with a health and safety remit or specific remit in relation to violence at work.

   - Training of staff to ensure that they can fulfil their responsibilities under the policy and protect themselves from violence at work.

7. **What is required of individuals**. This section could contain a general statement outlining the obligation of employees to take reasonable care of themselves and other people who may be affected by their acts or omissions.

   Other areas this section could cover include the following:

   - The requirement to operate procedures as laid down, such as entry procedures, wearing of badges, notification to reception of visitors expected, booking in and out of the workplace, use of a diary system and so on.

   - Attendance at training events such as those concerned with the policy, the implementation of procedures, systems such as reporting of incidents of violence or more specialist events for managers, front-line staff, travelling staff or other groups.

- Reporting of incidents of violence using the procedures available to them.

- The particular roles of individuals, e.g. supervisors, line managers, personnel staff, safety or welfare staff and training staff.

- Reporting of hazards, risks or problems that individuals identify or become aware of in the course of their work.

8. **Performance measures**. The inclusion of performance measures within the policy means that the effectiveness of the policy can be assessed against them. Performance measures include:

- A reduction in the number of incidents, attacks, assaults or injuries over a given period.

- A reduction in the proportion of staff assaulted in a given time or particular area of work.

- A reduction in the number of working days lost as a consequence of incidents of violence.

- Fewer staff feeling concerned or afraid of violence at work or a raised level of morale (this may require a survey or other analysis before and after the implementation of the policy so that comparisons can be made).

- A reduction in the rate of increase in incidents of violence to staff.

- Fewer staff leaving because of fears of violence or actual violence (exit interviews are one way of gathering this information).

- Reductions in compensation claims or payments or insurance premiums.

- Increase in productivity.

Performance measures can be developed for the whole organization, parts of it or specific types of work. They are particularly useful in assessing the effectiveness of newly developed procedures.

Performance measures that can help to demonstrate effects such as fewer working days lost, higher morale, greater productivity or lower turnover of staff assist in justifying the costs of security equipment, providing transport, changing procedures or other measures taken to combat violence at work.

9. **Evaluation/review**. The policy itself should include information about how its effectiveness will be assessed. This may be details of who will take responsibility, when assessment will take place, the process that will be used and how the results will be communicated to people and acted on.

Similar methods to those used in investigating the risks of violence at work (Chapter 4) can be used in evaluation including questionnaires, group meetings, observation and structured interviews.

An evaluation process based directly on assessment against performance measures within the policy can be developed. Evaluation data can also be obtained from data generated by other systems such as personnel systems, for example, staff turnover figures, exit interview reports or fewer problems in recruiting staff.

In addition, when a violence at work incident report system is in place this will provide direct data on the scale of the problem and any changes in it, including an increase or decrease in people seeking some sort of aftercare.

51

Finally, in developing a new policy it is wise to incorporate the first review date into the policy to ensure that it does actually happen. Thereafter reviews should be at regular intervals but not necessarily very frequent.

IMPLEMENTING POLICY – DEVELOPING PROCEDURES

Developing and agreeing a policy is a vital step towards a coherent organizational response to violence at work, but it is only one step. Policies often stop at the point where they are statements of intent and, while the intentions are good, little action follows because of the lack of procedures.

The policy itself says what people will do; the procedures then go on to say how they will do things. The procedures required will depend on what the policy says, the nature and scale of the problem of violence at work in the organization and the organization itself in terms of size, culture and the nature of its work.

The sorts of procedure that may be required include the following:

- procedures that detail how particular jobs or tasks should be performed, e.g.

    - reception duties;
    - taking cash to the bank or collecting cash;
    - interviewing members of the public;

- procedures may deal with working practices such as:

    - notification of and receiving visitors;
    - wearing of identification badges;
    - controlling access to buildings or parts of them;

- procedures related to working patterns, e.g.

    - working out of the office and the use of diary sheets, signing-in and -out systems;
    - security procedures when working late;
    - working in other people's homes or premises;
    - travelling on business;

- procedures for obtaining security equipment including:

    - mobile telephones/car telephones;
    - personal alarms;
    - two-way radios;

- procedures for dealing with tradespeople, contractors and deliveries:

    - nominated contact person in charge of people working on premises;
    - checks or vetting of people who will work in the organization;
    - reception of people into the organization and systems for identifying them while they are working;

- procedures for training in support of the policy such as:
    - induction;
    - general health and safety;

- communication skills;
- interpersonal skills;
- assertiveness training;
- how to operate procedures;
- practical techniques for protection;
- specialist training, e.g. counselling;
- managers – on their roles in policy implementation;

- procedures for monitoring incidents of violence, including:

  - a reporting system;
  - a report form;
  - a nominated member of staff responsible for reports and monitoring information;
  - the use of monitoring information;

- procedure for following up incidents of violence and providing aftercare for victims, e.g.

  - actions the organization will take to assist victims directly, such as time off work, protected earnings;
  - services the organization will obtain for victims, e.g. counselling;
  - support available for victims, e.g. legal advice, medical assistance;

- procedures for routine safety checking such as:
  - locking up, keyholders, setting alarms;
  - testing of safety equipment ;
  - maintenance and repair of safety equipment or systems;
  - reporting faults or risks to people responsible for safety precautions;

- procedures for evaluation/review of the policy including:

  - when they will take place;
  - who is responsible for evaluation and review and how it will be done;
  - how the results will be communicated.

6
Reporting Violent Incidents

Reporting systems can themselves be part of an investigation of risks at work where they already exist or they may be developed as part of the procedures for implementing policy.

Some organizations use existing accident report systems to record incidents of violence. This system is not generally used unless actual injury results from the incident so it can give a false picture of the level of violent incidents and lead to a false sense of security.

A separate system using a form to record violent incidents usually works best. A simple form that can be completed by, or on behalf of, a victim provides information that can be analysed and used in the development of future preventative measures.

Useful information to collect on the form includes:

- time, day and date of the incident, as this may help identify peak periods of risk, patterns of incidents at certain times or people at risk because of the times they work;

- a sketch or description of the location of the incident can sometimes help identify design flaws that can be rectified;

- an account of what happened leading up to and during the incident can, for example, highlight a need for back-up staff or security staff, indicate where normal practice leaves staff vulnerable to attack, suggest that alarms or panic button systems are required or that training is required to help staff operate existing procedures or develop skills in managing potentially violent people;

- asking the victim to describe the attacker can sometimes help identify particular sections of the public who represent a risk to staff;

- attempting to identify causes and motives may help to suggest where systems and procedures trigger violence, e.g.

  - when people have been kept waiting;
  - where people cannot get access to whom they believe can help;
  - when documentation or letters are not understood;
  - when someone tries to grab money within sight and/or reach;

- the name and details of the victim, although you may decide that forms can be completed anonymously.

Once a form has been designed it is best to start using it, practise with it to see how well it works and, as you learn more about the information it actually collects, redesign it if necessary.

54

As the report of the incident is not the end of the matter you may wish to keep records of the effects of the incident on the victim and property as well as details of follow-up actions taken and aftercare for the victim. This information can be kept separately or on the reverse of the incident report form and completed by the person responsible, e.g. personnel manager, safety officer or nominated manager.

The incident report form must remain confidential; people will not feel inclined to report incidents unless they feel sure that their privacy will be protected.

Monitoring information or details for management reports can still be extracted from the incident report forms without identifying victims.

It is essential that all employees are aware of the procedures for reporting violent incidents. They need to know:

- who is the person with overall responsibility for the procedure;

- how to obtain an incident report form;

- how to complete the form or where to get help if they cannot complete it;

- what to do with the completed form;

- whom to go to for advice, help and support or any of the aftercare services;

- how they will receive information about any follow-up action taken.

Following are examples of incident report forms.

Confidential   **Page one**

INCIDENT REPORT FORM   **Ref no.**

Employee

Name   Job title

Department/site/section

When did the incident occur?

Date   Day   Time

Assailant/s

Name (if known)

Address (if known)

Other contact point (e.g. workplace)

Approx. age   Sex

Description (physical and manner, e.g. drunk)

Where did the incident occur? (Draw a sketch if necessary)

What actually happened leading up to and during the incident?
(Attach a separate sheet if needed)

Probable motive or cause for the attack

Names of any witnesses

This page to be completed by personnel   **Page two**

INCIDENT REPORT FORM   **Ref no.**

Outcome of incident

Effect on victim (e.g. injury, time off work, psychological effects)

Damage to personal property

Damage to company property

Details of follow-up action taken and aftercare

Police

Legal action

Hospital treatment

Counselling

Specialist care

Victim support

Line manager/supervisor

Personnel

Health and safety officer

Security

Trade union

CONFIDENTIAL

KEEP IN EMPLOYEE'S FILE WITH ASSOCIATED COMMUNICATIONS

MONITORING DATA ONLY TO MONITORING FILE

Confidential

INCIDENT REPORT FORM

Date/day/time of incident

Employee

Name

Address

Job/grade   Department

Assailant/s

Name/s

Address/es

Age   Male/female

Any other details known

The incident   Give an account of the incident and details of any relevant events leading
to it

Outcome

(1)   Injury, verbal abuse, damage to property

(2)   Time lost, legal action, aftercare

Location of incident   Provide a sketch if possible

Any other relevant information   Include any witnesses

58

7
Aftercare – Helping and Supporting Victims

The most sophisticated policies and procedures for safety adopted by organizations cannot guarantee that a violent incident will never occur.

Since it is impossible to guarantee safety, the development of 'aftercare' services that will be available to anyone who does become a victim of violence is a sensible step. Such services ensure the organization is able to respond in terms of providing support, practical help and access to sources of specialist help if required.

Some of the aftercare services that could be developed are outlined below.

DEBRIEFING

Research shows that people who have been victims of violence need to talk through their experience as soon as possible after the event if long-term trauma is to be avoided. The initial step is to identify people in the organization who will undertake the debriefing (e.g. personnel staff, health or welfare staff, line managers) and train them. Everyone in the organization then needs to know who has been trained for this task and how to contact them. They must be contactable quickly and able to give immediate priority to requests for debriefing at any time.

Important points for a debriefer to remember are:

- Verbal abuse can be just as upsetting as a physical attack.

- Avoid any criticism of the employee's actions with the benefit of hindsight.

- What might have been or should have been done in this incident is less important than what can be learnt for the future to avoid a recurrence.

- A debriefer's role is to listen, support and encourage the victim to talk; do not expect to 'solve' anything at this stage.

- Debriefers need to know their limits and when and how it is more appropriate to ask for specialist help.

- Debriefers are not meant to be expert counsellors or psychologists; they are the immediate, first line help in a process that may go on for some time in some cases.

Debriefing may be a suitable way of providing immediate help for some victims while others may need specialist help from the outset. The aftercare services need to recognize this and not assume debriefing will be adequate in all cases.

The knowledge that the organization takes incidents of violence seriously enough to assign and train people as debriefers can encourage employees to report incidents and get the help they need quickly.

COUNSELLING

Some victims may need specialist help or help over a much longer period that cannot be provided by people within the organization.

Some organizations do have internal counselling services, though not many. Others have identified counselling services locally that they can call on when required. However, most organizations will probably need to identify a counsellor if and when the need arises. Counsellors can be identified in a numbers of ways such as through general practitioners, victim support schemes, local hospitals and the British Association of Counselling.

Providing professional counselling is sometimes an essential part of helping people to go through the process of acknowledging what has happened to them, adapting to it and being able to move on.

While it will take time and money to provide counselling services this is a small investment if it avoids future problems for the individual and enables him/her to return to work and to be effective.

VISITING VICTIMS

When victims are off work recovering it is important to keep in touch with them because they may

- need debriefing;

- need other help that the organization can identify and/or supply;

- want to feel they are still in touch with work;

- want to know what has happened as a result of the incident;

- need to be reassured that people care about them and do not blame them in any way for what has happened.

When considering visiting victims it is well worth finding out whom the victim would like to see and when they would like to see them. Some victims may need a few days to come to terms with what has happened to them, or reflect on the incident before seeing people from the workplace.

TIME OFF WORK

Employees who are physically injured as a result of violence obviously need time off work to recover. Some people who suffer no physical injury need time off work too: they may need to come to terms with what happened, recover from shock or regain their confidence; other people may prefer to go straight back to work.

Employers need to consider how time off work following incidents of violence will be managed. They may decide to set an allowance to apply in all cases or to develop a 'sliding scale' of time off allowed in different circumstances or take each individual case on its merits.

Dealing with each case individually recognizes that everyone is different, will react differently and will need differing amounts of time to recover. Although this approach can be more difficult to manage than a policy that gives everyone X days, it will enable victims to feel comfortable about recovering at their own pace or taking sufficient time to recover fully. It may also avoid victims suffering any physical or psychological problems in the future as a result of returning to work too quickly.

PROTECTED EARNINGS

Any employee who has to have time off work will be likely to be concerned about loss of earnings. This could be loss of earnings as a direct result of being off work for a long time or indirectly because, while paid their wage or salary, they miss out on bonus or overtime payments.

Reasonable employers would generally take the view that employees who become victims of violence in the line of duty should not suffer financially as well.

How employers manage the problems of earnings will very much depend on the particular circumstances and systems for payments within the organization. In cases where a straightforward monthly salary or weekly wage is paid this could simply be guaranteed. Where bonus payments or overtime are involved it may be necessary to work out an average over a period before the incident and guarantee it per month or per week while the employee is off work.

Unlike the case of time off work it may well be better to have a very clear policy on protecting earnings so that it can be communicated to all employees and they can know exactly what to expect. A policy also avoids the risk of any unfair treatment based on judgements that would have to be made in an ad hoc system.

LEGAL HELP

The sort of legal help an employee may require will depend on the nature of the violent incident and the consequences of it. In some cases the police will bring a prosecution, and while this has the advantage of costing the victim nothing directly, he/she may get nothing in the form of compensation from it. There could be costs attached if the victim is to give evidence and the organization could help with this and/or make good any loss of property or goods the victim suffered. In addition information and support from a legal department or solicitor conversant with the proceedings could help the victim in the potentially traumatic business of giving evidence.

When the police do not bring a prosecution there may still be scope for the individual to bring a civil action. In the first instance the organization could secure legal advice on behalf of the employee as to whether or not a civil action is likely to be successful in the circumstances.

Bringing a civil action can be very costly and organizations should consider to what extent they can assist in bringing such actions, in what circumstances and the terms of such an arrangement.

Where personal injuries have been sustained by a victim in the UK that are directly attributable to a crime of violence, application can be made for an award from the Criminal Injuries Compensation Board (who administer the Criminal Injury Compensation Scheme). The procedures are complex and organizations could offer help and advice through legal departments or their solicitors to employees who wish to make an application.

OTHER STAFF

If someone has been a victim of violence, whether or not they have been away from work, other staff can be helped to react appropriately if given some guidelines, for example:

- Our natural curiosity can get the better of us at times; staff should be asking 'how are you?' rather than 'what happened?'

- By all means show concern for the victim but be aware that he/she may not be ready or able to discuss feelings or the incident.

- If a victim does want to talk, let them; also let them be in control of what they tell you. Ask questions sensitively and do not probe if they are reticent.

- When the victim wants to stop talking do not persist.

- Do not criticize the action the victim describes taking or not taking in the incident.

- If you are at all concerned about the victim suggest someone trained to whom they should speak; if you do not believe they can do this but are in need of help you should speak to someone yourself, for example a line manager or personnel staff.

8
Taking Control

Taking control is about managing tension; the physical and mental effects of our feelings and emotions.

We may experience tension as a consequence of emotions such as fear and anxiety, anger, resentment or frustration; it may be as a result of what is commonly called stress or because we are overtired or unfit.

Tension can lead to a much lower tolerance level and increase an individual's potential for aggressive or violent behaviour. In addition tension can reduce the ability to cope with aggression or violence because it either causes people to react equally aggressively and escalate the situation or makes them unable to take the necessary action to remain safe in threatening situations.

First we look at some of the causes of tension, then at tension itself and, finally, some techniques for managing it.

FEAR

Fear, or anxiety, is a very basic, natural and necessary emotion; its function is to protect us from danger. Fear is the body's built-in alarm system, a biochemical system that prepares the body to deal with the threat or 'fright' by either 'fight' or 'flight' through the release of hormones. Through the nervous system two counterbalancing sub-systems are activated: the sympathetic and the parasympathetic. The former prepares the body for immediate or vigorous activity while the latter enables the body to conserve strength and relax. The normal state is one in which the two sub-systems are in balance, but, when faced with danger or threat, the sympathetic system becomes prominent and the body is geared for rapid responses.

Unlike animals people often grow up and are socialized in such a way that their instincts are modified or subdued; they come to believe that fear is negative, cowardly or 'sissy'. In fact fear is a very positive instinct that warns us when something is or may be wrong or threatening, giving us the opportunity to act very quickly to ensure our own safety.

Fear can be a much more reliable danger warning than is often acknowledged. As rational, socialized human beings our tendency is often not to act on instinct but to assess the situation, analyse the source of our feelings and decide on a course of action. This may not always be very wise. Acknowledging and acting on the early feelings of fear can be a form of taking control rather than giving in. If your fear turns out to be unfounded you may feel silly but at least you are safe.

If you ignore the early warning signs the threat, and your fear, may increase to an extreme point where you freeze, stop thinking or even stop breathing and pass out.

Clearly most daily work situations are not extreme cases of threat and thus you are more likely to be able to consider the situation you face rather than fight or take flight immediately. However, even in the work setting it is important to be able to recognize and acknowledge when you feel fear in order to be able to take appropriate action to identify and deal with the cause or source of the feelings.

Each of us will respond to danger or threat and experience fear in our own particular way. Some of the physical reactions to fear are:

- tightening or churning of the stomach, or 'butterflies'

- cold hands and feet

- sweaty palms, forehead or top lip

- increase in heartbeat

- difficulty in breathing, or holding breath

- tightening of muscles such as jaw muscles; spine going rigid, shoulders hunch or stiffen

- wobbly legs

- dry mouth and difficulty in speaking.

Perhaps the most common physical reaction to fear is when your hair 'stands on end' and there is a creeping sensation in your skin. It is quite hard to see this effect on people because we have little body hair, but it is easy to recognize if you look at a cat with its back arched, the hair along its spine standing on end and its tail swelled up as the hairs stand out from it.

It is these physical responses to the emotion of fear that we experience as tension. The tension is necessary, both physically and mentally, if we are to be able to 'fight' or 'take flight' when and if the need arises because it prepares us for such rapid action.

The tension becomes a problem when it is extreme: you freeze, cannot think or speak, when it is sustained at a high level. Because it is not discharged it can become physically or mentally damaging.

Learning to manage or control the tension arising from fear makes it much more likely that you will be able to do something positive about the source of the fear such as run away, develop avoidance strategies so it does not happen again or stand your ground having decided how to tackle the situation.

ANGER

Anger is probably the emotion that most of us repress most often. Whether we are cross, frustrated, resentful or blazing mad it is often very difficult to express the feelings and let others know how we feel because culturally or socially it seems unacceptable to do so.

64

Anger is not always bad; expressing feelings of anger at an early stage can sometimes avoid situations escalating or frustration and resentment building up.

The effect of repressed anger can be that the tension builds up to such a point that some people lose control and 'blow their tops' while others become introverted, cowed or dejected. In either case there is a risk that they will become violent themselves or meet violence with violence so that, in lashing out, nasty situations become dangerous.

Simmering anger, frustration or resentment can lead to covert attempts to 'get your own back', where people have become inward-looking, focusing on their own feelings and coming to regard others increasingly as a threat or deserving of the same kind of treatment they have had.

When people are faced with bureaucracy or are unable to have their needs met, or when blocks are put in their way or their problems minimized it is not difficult to see why the build-up of tension is such that it explodes as violent behaviour. The most serious forms of violence are often preceded by strong feelings of anger and the build-up of tension. Angry situations generally develop through four stages:

1. Trigger

2. Interpretation

3. Arousal

4. Behaviour

The **trigger** can be something you feel you must achieve or do, something you must resolve now or get an answer to or a problem you want solved.

> Imagine you are sitting in your office trying to finish an urgent and important report you have been struggling with. The people in the next office are making a row, laughing and joking again; you have already asked them several times to be quiet.

Interpretation is about how the person perceives or understands the actions of the other person or people. They read into the actions of the other people meaning or intentions that may or may not be accurate, for example:

> The people in the next office know you are up for promotion and that your report will be carefully scrutinized; they have always resented your progress; they do not take their jobs seriously.

Arousal describes the tension developing both physically and psychologically.

> As the noise and laughter from the next office intrudes further into your thoughts you get more and more annoyed and agitated and become angry. You set your jaw, clench your fists, start to sweat and your heart races as you get to your feet.

Behaviour is the action then taken.

> You go to the next-door office, fling open the door, storm in shouting and screaming at people and accusing them of deliberately upsetting you, trying to distract you, being jealous of you and so on.

The result of all this is a confrontation that could well degenerate into violent behaviour on either side.

Clearly the same process can be operating in situations that lead to much more serious consequences than is usual at work, for example actual bodily harm or murder. The same process can also be identified when clients or customers come seeking advice, help or service and are confronted with what they interpret as unwillingness or an inability to meet their needs and so the interaction degenerates into violent behaviour.

Developing the skill of managing the tension set up by anger can help you in a number of ways, for example:

- It can help you to find ways of expressing feelings and doing something about them before they build up into uncontrollable anger and boil over.

- If you are really angry it can help you to recognize the risk of lashing out or exploding and enable you to harness the tension and use it to go and tackle the source of your problem more appropriately.

- It can help you to recognize the build-up of anger and tension in others and adopt appropriate strategies for calming the situation, avoid behaviour that would escalate the situation or simply give you warning of danger and time to get away.

STRESS

If you ask people what they mean by stress you will get a great variety of answers. Among experts (doctors, psychologists) there still seems to be two broad ways of defining it. There are those who say stress is a demand on our energy; it is what gets us going physically and mentally and without it we would make little progress or get bored. There are others who define stress as any interference that disturbs a person's healthy mental state and physical well-being.

Probably both these definitions together give the most accurate picture of stress. We all need the right amount of stress, in the sense of demands on our energy, to keep us active, busy, lively, interested, contributing and feeling valued and useful. If we had no demands on our energy we would soon become bored, lethargic and have little sense of self-worth or self-esteem. This has been demonstrated both in experiments and in real-life situations (e.g. hostages) where people have been deprived of the demands, challenges or environmental stimuli of everyday life and all are affected; some become seriously disturbed.

On the other hand too many demands, especially competing demands, on our energy can disturb our mental and physical well-being too. We can become overtired, anxious, hyperactive, stop eating or suffer from a whole range of reactions to or side effects of the stress.

When people are faced with stressful situations the body responds by increasing the production of the hormones cortisol and adrenaline. Stress acts on the nervous system causing blood vessels to constrict, changes in the heart rate, a rise in blood pressure, changes in the metabolism and preparation for physical activity designed to improve overall performance. This response is intended to get us ready for action and is necessary and functional. When people suffer from stress they are in this heightened state of preparedness, or tension, for too long or too often and the result can be unpleasant physical and/or psychological side-effects.

It is a question of balance. We all need stress to a degree but beyond a certain point it can be harmful. Everyone is different: the degree of stress they need and the point at which that becomes 'over-stress' will vary from person to person. When stress becomes 'over-stress' may well depend on what is happening to an individual at the time. There are certain life events recognized as putting people under pressure including marriage, divorce, birth, changing jobs, moving house, bereavement and illness. At these, or other stressful times in life, people's stress tolerance may be significantly different from other times.

There are different types of stress, for example:

- Stress can be hidden or unconscious, such as feelings of annoyance or resentment people have towards other people because of something they did, did not do or some past injustice. This sort of stress can be unrecognized for some time but it can affect relationships, performance at work or general health.

- Unnoticed stress usually occurs when we are doing something familiar, quite often over long periods and sometimes thinking of something else at the same time. Examples include: motorway driving where drivers can have a very high pulse rate for long periods; working through detailed checking procedures on figures or reports, leading to tension.

- There are also obvious feelings of stress that people experience when having to do things like present a report, go for an interview, conduct a negotiation, discipline someone or deal with angry customers.

The symptoms of stress will vary from person to person and they may be physical or psychological or both. People experience physical reactions such as a feeling of general debility, fatigue, loss of appetite, palpitations, indigestion, muscular aches and pains, headaches, abdominal cramps and insomnia.

Other symptoms of stress include irritability, depression, anxiety, nightmares, apprehension, poor concentration, feelings of being unable to cope, loss of self worth, guilt and anger. As well as physical and psychological changes, overstress can lead to quite marked changes in behaviour. People who would not normally dream of doing so react to stress by:

- disregarding tasks even though they are important or have a high priority;

- blocking out new information or avoiding new situations;

- becoming distant or detached from situations;

- falling behind with work;

- failing to attend meetings, events, conferences;

- developing a 'don't care' attitude;

- losing interest and energy;

- feeling little motivation.

Perhaps the most extreme example of what can happen to people when stress becomes overstress is 'burnout'. 'Burnout' is a term coined in the United States in the 1970s to describe a syndrome characterized by physical and emotional exhaustion and the development of negative feelings about self, jobs and others. While 'burnout' is recognizable in some people it is relatively rare.

Causes of stress at work

The causes of stress are often very complex and may be found in one's personality and personal life as well as working life, or indeed these aspects may be interrelated. Here we are concerned with the stress at work but it is important to acknowledge that some of the stresses we experience at work may actually have their causes elsewhere and no amount of time and effort devoted to changing the work situation will resolve the problem.

Some of the most common causes of stress at work include:

- Overload – having too much to do or too few hours in the day; when you feel too much is expected of you, or you expect too much of yourself. You feel you do nothing properly or well because there is just so much to get through. You are overwhelmed by

67

the quantity of work, the speed of work required and the conflicting demands on you or the conflicting priorities.

- Physical demands – physically strenuous work with little variety or let up in the demands on your strength and energy. You feel strained or you have to struggle. Chronic tiredness gets to the point where 'mind over matter' does not work any longer and you become physically incapable of performing.

- Emotional demands – some jobs carry with them the need to make difficult ethical decisions, constantly deal with problems or undertake unpleasant tasks such as disciplinary meetings, dismissing people or making them redundant. You may feel pressure from having to perform the tasks without having the time to do the job in a way you feel happy about; quantity takes over from quality.

- Night work – the internal 'body clock' regulates much of the body's physiology on a 24-hour cycle. Normally the rhythms put us in a waking mode with a higher body temperature, alertness and mental agility in the day; and a sleep mode with a decrease in body temperature and increase in fatigue at night. Day work matches the internal clock and our activities in the external environment; night work does the opposite. In addition the demands of personal life and the activity of daytime can make it difficult to sleep. Thus night workers can become out of rhythm with their body clock and with the lives of those around them.

- Change – organizational change, reorganization, mergers and the restructuring of work are all recognized as causes of stress at work. Not knowing what is going on, feeling threatened or deskilled, a sense of insecurity or fear of the unknown are all common reactions to change. Change need not be on a vast scale to cause stress; a new manager, changed performance standards or targets or new procedures often result in increased stress levels although the change is relatively minor.

- Responsibility – you can feel responsibility is pushed on to you when it is not really yours; you may not wish to accept new responsibilities but fear the consequences of refusing; you could be made responsible without being given the power to fulfil the responsibility or you may feel ill-equipped or trained for your responsibilities but fear saying so. Lack of clarity about where responsibility lies can cause confusion and stress. Balancing responsibilities and establishing priorities between them can be stressful.

- Home/work conflict – balancing work, home, family, other care responsibilities and personal commitments or interests can feel like juggling two or more full-time jobs and makes an enormous demand on energy. What happens at home can affect work and vice versa. Home responsibilities may seem to get in the way of career for some, while others will feel work encroaches increasingly into their personal life and they seem to be neglecting home.

- Organizational culture – the organizational culture may be very competitive and fast-moving, forcing you to go with it or get left behind. A culture may be such that it does not value communication, support or feedback so you feel isolated, not knowing what is going on, not sure about how well or badly you are performing or not knowing where or how to get help. Some cultures can be so concerned with the 'process' that the 'task' gets neglected; in these situations people can become frustrated and bored, irritated by all the talking and little action.

- Interpersonal relationships – coping with difficult employees, employers, situations, clients or members of the public creates stress. Poor relationships with colleagues, work teams or groups that do not function or unresolved interpersonal conflict results in a stressful atmosphere. The feeling that managers do not listen or understand creates a sense of being undervalued. Colleagues who are negative or want to sabotage work generate frustration and resentment.

(See pages 76–79 for practical tips on starting to tackle each of these areas.)

Stress can result from or give rise to all sorts of emotions ranging from anger to depression. We all react differently to the types of stresses and strains we experience in our working lives and to the tension that sets up.

Learning to manage the tension can help in identifying the causes of stress, tackling the source of the stress we experience, controlling our own behaviour and in preventing stress levels reaching a point where they become physically or psychologically damaging.

TENSION

Tension is a way of describing the effects on the body of feelings and emotions. We often assume that tension is not good for us but, like most things, it is not all bad. Without some tension you would not be able to breathe, think, speak, keep upright or be lively and alert. Muscles need 'tone' to support the skeleton and to move limbs; you need the release of hormones to get your nervous system and brain going so that you can think, communicate, anticipate and react. Some tension is necessary to heighten awareness, feelings and the enjoyment of life.

What is not good is constant or excessive tension, where our reactions are so intense or prolonged that they can not only cause short-term behavioural problems but can eventually result in physical damage. At the very least excesses of tension adversely affect performance, one's sense of well-being and the quality of life.

The main purpose of tension is to put us in a state of readiness to respond to danger, threat or risk. It comes about when our senses, mainly eyes and ears, receive an alarm signal of some sort. The signal need not necessarily be of the kind that suggests you are in imminent physical danger (e.g. someone following you at night); it could be a signal such as the appearance of someone suggesting trouble or the actions or words of people at work triggering feelings of being undervalued or treated unfairly. The signal is passed on to the brain which recognizes its significance and sends out messages via the nervous system to the muscles. The tensing sensation you sometimes feel, as when something makes you jump, can be the effect of muscles contracting rapidly in response to those signals. The body is then on full alert and ready for action.

The signal via the senses to the brain, nervous system and then the muscles which contract into tension, triggers a series of changes in the body:

- a changed heart rate: normally it will increase, as it may when you are startled. On some occasions, in anticipation of something unpleasant, the heart beat slows and the beating feels very strong;

- a rise in blood pressure, sometimes to a very high level and/or for long periods;

- changes in blood vessels: those in the muscles open up to let more blood through; those in the abdomen and skin contract and less blood goes through. Blood from the heart is diverted to the muscles to aid muscular effort; the effect elsewhere can be that your skin becomes very pale and you get a 'sinking' feeling in your tummy;

- sweating increases, mainly around the mouth and nose, the temples, armpits, between the legs and especially the soles of the feet and palms of the hands;

69

- drying up of saliva accompanied by an increase in the secretion of gastric acid. The intestines may churn and gurgle, you may feel the need to go to the toilet;

- dilation of the pupils so that more light is let into your eyes and they are helped to become more sensitive. Your other senses are similarly affected so that their sensitivity increases;

- an expansion of the tubes to your lungs which allows more air to be drawn in more quickly;

- a change in hormones, principally an increase in adrenalin, noradrenalin, cortisol and hydrocortisone. These hormones act on many organs and reinforce all the above effects. In addition, adrenalin influences the metabolic balance of the body, mobilizing energy reserves in the liver and in the muscles themselves, making glucose available to meet immediate demands for energy.

This state of alertness is ideal for dealing with situations of risk or danger where you need to spring quickly into action or use speed or strength to respond. If you do have to react in this way, once you are safe again or your task is complete, the tension subsides as the body returns to a more balanced, relaxed state.

If it was a false alarm, once you are sure it was a false alarm you will relax and gradually the effects of tension will subside.

However, there are times when the body is fully prepared and ready for action, the tension has set in motion all the alert responses but there is no means of discharging them because the fight or flight responses would be inappropriate. Such situations can arise at work, for example:

- You negotiate agreements with the trade union on practices and procedures and everyone is in agreement, yet, when it comes to it, you get no support from your senior managers who continue to do what they like and leave you to cope with irate unions and the problems and complaints from staff. You end up having to toe the management line and manage the unpleasant consequences of their actions as well.

- Whenever you submit proposals to your boss to go to the Board they are turned down but you have no direct access to the Board to do anything about it; you just have to grin and bear it and draft them again.

Other situations that can leave you with no outlet for your responses include those times when decisions are taken around you or despite you by others more powerful; when bosses impose unrealistic targets and deadlines or when customers or clients you dare not lose treat you badly or make impossible demands. As a consequence of these and similar situations where you cannot burn off the reactions, you are left with all the added chemicals flooding your body. Moreover you may then pick up further 'signals' to which you react so the process towards a state of alertness is repeated, adding to or maintaining the chemical inbalance so that you are in a constant state of tension or at least a very prolonged one.

When tension reaches levels that our bodies cannot cope with or are becoming potentially damaging a series of physical or psychological warning signals are set off. Each of us will have different warning signals or patterns of them and they may include:

- Physical symptoms:
  - throbbing head or headache
  - grinding teeth
  - twitches – especially of the eyes
  - tremulous voice
  - pain around the back of the head and neck

70

- tightness in the throat
- hyperventilation
- nail biting
- twiddling thumbs or fiddling
- palpitations, chest discomfort
- skin rashes
- feeling nauseous – vomiting
- indigestion
- diarrhoea or frequent urination
- backache, especially of lower back
- tiredness
- sweating
- trembling
- general debility or weakness
- breathlessness
- fainting.

- Psychological symptoms:
  - increase in smoking
  - increase in drinking alcohol
  - marked increase or decrease in appetite
  - constant desire and ability to sleep or insomnia
  - tiredness to the point of exhaustion
  - loss of sex drive
  - absent-mindedness, lack of concentration
  - inefficiency
  - loss of interest
  - feeling unable to cope
  - irritability
  - impulsiveness
  - lack of coordination
  - depression
  - lack of self-esteem and self-worth
  - hopelessness
  - guilt
  - anxiety.

All these can be reactions to tension; they are likely to be warnings that an excess of tension is causing your body to suffer illness unless of course they are symptoms of an illness you know you have. These reactions are generally unpleasant but they are useful in letting us know it is time to take action to manage or control the tension before it becomes damaging.

RELAXATION – TENSION CONTROL

There are clearly links between our feelings, stress and the tension they set up and there are also links between tension and violent behaviour.

71

Relaxation techniques are a means of managing tension so that:

- we can control our own tension and avoid aggressive or violent behaviour ourselves;

- we are able to control the physical and psychological effects of tension so that we can make choices and decisions that keep us safe in potentially dangerous circumstances;

- we recognize the danger signals from other people as their tension rises and can keep control of ourselves, avoid escalating the situation and even defuse it altogether.

Some suggestions as to how you can learn to control tension follow.

Quick relaxation of tension

This is a useful technique if you find yourself in a situation that is threatening or you find yourself tensing up for some other reason. In cases of serious threat you could find yourself freezing, unable to think or breathe, or even passing out. This quick relaxation technique will stop the tension response taking over and help you to react in a way that will ensure your safety. The rules are as follows:

- Do not tell yourself to relax. If you try the 'I must relax' approach you are likely to tense up still further.

- You have to practise the technique as if it is not natural; it is the natural reaction you want to learn to control.

- Learn to recognize the signals and know your own body and how you experience tension.

- As soon as you feel tension of any kind, deliberately tense up your muscles even more and then release the tension completely.

- Breathing properly is the key to relaxation. It is vital to concentrate on breathing out so you expel all the air and create a vacuum which will refill as a reflex action. If you concentrate on breathing in your tension may increase and the muscles of your chest contract. This will make breathing more difficult and, under extreme pressure, can lead to hyperventilating.

- Proper breathing also ensures a regular supply of oxygen to the brain to allow you to think clearly. It also keeps vocal chords open in case you need to scream or shout.

- Remember the tension you experience in the exercises is voluntary: you create it, but you are learning to deal with tension resulting from interactions with others.

- You have to keep practising even if it feels silly; once learned the technique does work.

How to practise
Sitting comfortably in a straight backed chair:

- Clench your hand into a fist until you feel your nails digging into your palms and you can see the whiteness of your knuckles.

- Release completely, including relaxing your arms, shoulders, neck and jaw.

- With your back against the chair back stretch your arms and outstretched hands along your thighs until your tensed fingers rise at the tips.

- Release completely, relaxing fingers, hands, arms, shoulders, neck, back.

- Push your shoulders downwards as hard as possible as if trying to push yourself into the seat of the chair; hold it.

- Release completely as before, relaxing your body into a comfortable sitting position.

- Push your back into the back of the chair and your heels into the floor as hard as you can using your leg muscles.

- Release again completely, relaxing the muscles of limbs and trunk.

- Expel all your breath in a deep sigh until your lungs feel empty.

- Relax so that you feel your lungs refill with air as a reflex action.

Repeat the routine above until you are sure you recognize the sensation of tension and of relaxation. Keep practising the routine so that you can feel the tension and relaxation but so that it is almost unseen or unrecognizable to people around you.

Once you feel able, practise the tension and relaxation while standing, talking to someone or with someone being difficult. Your aim is to be able to use the relaxation part of the exercise when the tension you experience is involuntary because it is triggered by someone or something other than you, so relaxation has to become almost second nature.

Long-term relaxation

Memorizing a relaxation technique may sound difficult but it is possible to learn the various elements gradually so that you become familiar with them over a period. Once you are familiar with the routine of tension control techniques your body will begin to respond automatically and eventually you will find yourself putting the technique into operation with little conscious effort. To reach this stage you do have to practise: it takes some concentration, time and effort to develop the skills. Relaxation is not a natural reaction in situations that are uncomfortable, threatening, distressing or difficult, so it is a skill that has to be learned.

How to practise

The following exercise will help you to learn how to control tension and relax in the longer term. To learn the tension control technique you need to take it step by step:

- Start by reading the instructions and doing each part of the exercise.

- Keep practising the exercise until you easily recognize tension and relaxation in the various muscles.

- Practise the exercises until you can remember them.

- Try using the exercises consciously (or some of them) when you are in a difficult or stressful situation.

- Continue to practise the exercises so that you feel confident you can use the technique almost automatically if you need to.

The tension control technique works on the premise that only a fully contracted muscle will fully relax when it is released. Just as the brain sends signals to the muscles, so muscles send signals back to the brain and a tense muscle reinforces the message that there is risk, danger or an 'alert' of some kind to respond to. The result can be that the state of tension is reinforced or enhanced. Relaxed muscles will have the opposite effect and so allow you to take control both physically and mentally. While it is a simple idea its value lies in the fact that it works.

Before you start to practise the exercises:

- Make sure you allow yourself time so that you can feel the tension and the relaxation. Allow at least ten minutes to go through the exercises.

- Try to do the exercises alone in a quiet atmosphere where you can concentrate and won't be disturbed.

- Make sure you can breathe easily; avoid restricting clothing or sitting in a slumped position.

- Sit comfortably in a chair with an upright back; your back and shoulders should be supported, feet flat on the ground and your knees slightly apart. Let your arms hang loosely with your hands on your lap.

- When you first practise the exercises, before you know them, prop the instructions up on a table at a distance you can comfortably read from your relaxed position.

- Remember to keep breathing regularly and easily throughout.

Start at the forehead   Wrinkle up the skin and frown between the eyebrows . . . hold it . . . let it go and release. Now frown hard, involve the whole scalp, feel the tightness . . . hold hard . . . release completely, feel the tension in the scalp relax.

Now for the eyes   Screw them up just slightly, feel the wrinkles at the sides . . . hold it . . . let go and release. Screw them up more tightly until there is only a pinprick of light . . . hold . . . and release. Screw them up tightly until the nose and forehead are involved . . . hold hard . . . let go completely.

On to the mouth   Pull sideways slightly . . . feel the tension . . . release. Pull the mouth into a smile . . . hold it . . . let go and release completely. Draw the mouth into a grimace . . . hold it hard . . . let go and relax.

Now for the jaw   Clench the teeth together . . . now release. Clench the teeth and jaw very tightly . . . feel the tension . . . release completely so that the jaw drops, the mouth opens and the tongue falls back.

Next the shoulders   Lift slightly, hold . . . now drop. Raise the shoulders higher . . . hold them . . . release and let them fall back. Lift the shoulders to the ears . . . hold hard, let them go and feel the tension release.

On to the hands   Clench the hands into fists and feel your fingernails in the palms . . . hold . . . and release. Clench the hands hard until the knuckles show white and you feel the tension in your shoulders . . . hold hard . . . let go and feel the tension release.

Now your trunk   Push the small of your back into the chair and feel the abdomen tighten and your pelvis move . . . hold . . . release. Repeat, making the movement stronger . . . hold longer . . . let go completely and feel yourself sink into the chair.

Down to your feet   Push your heels into the ground, feel the tension in the calves and thighs . . . hold . . . let go. Press down hard . . . hold tight . . . release completely.

Continue to sit   for a moment concentrating on breathing in and expanding, holding the breath briefly and then expelling as a release.

When you have learnt the exercises sitting down you could try this exercise. Lie down somewhere warm and comfortable. Put a pillow under your neck and knees for support.

74

- Start by breathing steadily and easily.

- Lift your head and look at your toes . . . feel the tension and release . . . repeat.

- Start at the toes and tighten your calves, buttocks, hands, shoulders, face. Hold and release . . . repeat.

- Now close your eyes and think of nothing but the feelings while you go through the routine slowly and steadily.

As you become more practised you will begin to be aware whenever your muscles are under tension, and you will naturally tense and release them. There will be times when you need to take the actions deliberately, and that is when you will be really amazed at the results – such as a clear mind, quicker thought and the ability to deal with tricky situations without producing aggression either in yourself or other people.

Looking after yourself

Consciously taking care of yourself physically and psychologically helps avoid tension becoming a problem; it also enables you to manage any tension effectively by 'unwinding' and thus minimizing the risk of any long-term health problems as a result of constant tension.

Looking after yourself could include the following:

- Exercise – stress and tension release glucose and fatty acids into the body but these are not normally used up. The unused fat can then be laid down in arteries. Exercise is a way of using up this energy released into the bloodstream. Apart from that, exercise makes you feel better generally and more able to cope.

  Walk more often, adopting a good posture, looking forward and walking briskly with arms swinging gently in rhythm. Swimming is one of the best ways to achieve a fully exercised and relaxed body. Swimming is the most effective of activities for improving suppleness, stamina and strength; it also stretches the body as well as supporting it so there is no undue strain on any limbs or joints.

  Other sports can help too, such as squash, badminton, running, jogging and so on but it is important not to rush straight into strenuous exercise; take time to get used to it and increase your fitness, otherwise you can do more harm than good.

- Occupying your mind – finding things to do that are both relaxing and diverting can be an excellent means of controlling tension. Music is very soothing and calming; it can also be exhilarating and help release inhibitions. Dancing or singing can be especially helpful as they involve music and movement and thus use up the chemicals in the body left over from tension. Hobbies are also a form of diversion that can be as simple or complex as you choose. A hobby that does not make demands on you is more effective when it comes to reducing tension; avoid things that will make demands on you that you will find hard to refuse.

  Learn something new such as a language or take a night school course. Avoid situations where you feel pressurized to learn for an examination; choose something you can learn for yourself, at your pace, as and when you wish.

- Spoil yourself – one way of releasing tension or getting over tension is to think of yourself and find ways to pamper yourself and value yourself. Go for a massage; it is one of the most effective ways of achieving both physical and mental relaxation when done properly and in the right atmosphere.

75

Treat yourself to something you will enjoy and will make you feel good such as a facial, manicure or hairdo; or go out and buy something new to wear or treat yourself to a special meal.

- Diet – tension can often cause you to stop eating or to overeat or eat the wrong things. An inappropriate diet can also contribute to a state of health that makes you more prone to the effects of tension. Try to ensure that you have proper, balanced meals and that you make time to eat them. Eat more wholefoods and fewer refined foods. Avoid stimulants such as tea, coffee and alcohol. Find out if you have a reaction to, or an allergy to, particular foodstuffs. Try to select soothing drinks such as camomile tea and treat yourself to fruits rather than chocolates.

- Sleep – sleeping properly is essential to your well-being. Without proper sleep you can become nervous and tense and when you are anxious or stressed you can suffer from insomnia. It can become a vicious circle. Sleep not only refreshes the body it also, through dreams, restores the mind and discharges tension.

   If you find that you are tired but cannot sleep and are lying in bed tossing and turning there are a number of things you can do without resorting to sleeping pills. Exercise or activity that wears you out physically can help, so make sure you are physically active.

   Avoid alcohol because, while it can make you sleepy initially, it has a stimulating effect on the brain after an hour or so.

   Go through the relaxation exercises before going to bed so that you have physically relaxed.

   Have a long, relaxing bath and a soothing drink such as herb tea before bedtime.

   Lying in bed, comfortable, warm and relaxed, think about an occasion or event you thoroughly enjoyed and replay the event in detail and in sequence. Repeat the exercise filling in more detail as you go and savouring the memories of enjoying it.

   If you really cannot sleep do not lie there worrying; get up and do something enjoyable, active or interesting until you feel tired. A shorter period of proper sleep is better than fitful, restless sleep.

- Catharsis – there are times when the only effective way to deal with tension is to let it out. Try to do this in a way that will not harm you or others. Have a really good cry; thump or throw cushions about; get yourself a punch bag and punch it; smash old crockery or rip up old clothes; throw a tantrum or scream and shout into a pillow.

- Learn a technique – you can help develop skills of managing tension by learning techniques that are relaxing. Yoga is one example that can help both physically and mentally. Meditation can also help as it enables you to achieve a totally relaxed, calm or even trance-like state that reduces blood pressure and the physical effects of tension.

- Pets – animals can have a remarkably calming effect. Watching fish in a tank can be very soothing and relaxing. Stroking an animal that is both at rest and responsive to you has been shown to be a very effective way of calming, reducing blood pressure and aiding relaxation. Animals also make good companions: they are generally accepting and undemanding of anything other than food and affection and usually love you even if you are in a bad mood!

Managing Tension at Work

The following are some practical approaches to limiting the build-up of tension at work.

- Overload

  - set priorities and sensible timescales;
  - allow sufficient time for priority tasks and stick to it;
  - go somewhere else to work such as home or the library if you cannot work in your office;
  - avoid interruption and being sidetracked;
  - plan your activities and stick to the plan as far as possible. If you must balance your needs with those of other people acknowledge that your own needs are legitimate too;
  - be clear about the degree of control you have, use what you have and accept what you have not;
  - delegate where you can do so appropriately;
  - think of yourself and discipline yourself: if needs be become more punctual, more decisive, less accessible or willing to take on others' problems; do not assume you have to do everything – try to minimize 'down time' such as interruption, social chat, meetings that are not essential, time away;
  - think about how you might improve your management skills through having, for example, training in report writing, rapid reading, time management or managing meetings.

- Physical demands

  - make sure you find ways to keep fit;
  - eat properly and regularly;
  - take proper breaks and rest periods;
  - find ways of alternating strenuous with less strenuous work;
  - make sure equipment or machinery is not badly placed or poorly designed as this will create greater strain;
  - use mechanical aids to heavy work wherever possible;
  - get help with heavy jobs so as to limit strain;
  - suggest a rota system for sharing out the most strenuous tasks.

- Emotional demands

  - talk to people, share your feelings and uncertainties instead of bottling them up;
  - design group or team meetings so that there is time for people to exchange experiences and concerns and get support;
  - counselling help can be useful in dealing with emotional overload;
  - seek advice, help or support if needed rather than carrying problems alone;
  - try to identify further training that could help with the performance of emotionally demanding tasks.

- Night work

  - create regular patterns for yourself by going to bed, eating, getting up and so on at regular times;
  - try to sleep in as quiet an environment as possible; if you have to, use ear plugs;
  - if you wake too soon try to avoid becoming agitated: relax, turn over and go back to sleep;

77

- most people naturally have a sleepy period after lunch, about 2 pm; use that time to sleep if you need to;
- organize your leisure time around sleep and work so that you still have time for family, friends, appointments and so on and so avoid feeling you are neglecting people and tasks.

- Change

  - be clear about what is fixed or constant; establish certainty where possible;
  - share your concerns with other people and accept change is an uncomfortable process for everyone;
  - if you do not know, ask. Rumours are always rife at times of change so clear them up as soon as possible;
  - try to balance what you perceive as the threats of the change with the opportunities it may provide;
  - do not make a fight of it – if you know things must change find a role in bringing about the changes so that you have a part to play, an opportunity to influence the changes and a degree of control in the process.

- Responsibility

  - make sure you are clear about what is and is not your responsibility;
  - find a way to communicate to others what you are responsible for and what you are not responsible for;
  - if there is lack of clarity about your responsibilities you may need to renegotiate them with other people, perhaps using your job description as a vehicle to do this;
  - if you have responsibilities or are asked to take on responsibility make sure you can fulfil expectations and do what is required; if necessary seek training, support, advice and so on;
  - avoid taking on other people's responsibilities;
  - do not allow other people to 'dump' their responsibilities on you;
  - if additional responsibilities are being pushed your way consider your rights to have your job description changed, obtain help or back-up, to pass other work to other people or have your salary appropriately adjusted;
  - refuse the unfair giving of responsibility to you; it may take an effort but, if done assertively, can be a reasonable exercise of your rights.

- Home/work conflict

  - try to be clear about the boundaries between work and home, for example whether you will do overtime or weekend work; if or when you will take work home; what could happen at home that would take precedence over work;
  - discuss and/or negotiate agreed ways of working with managers, supervisors and colleagues;
  - discuss and/or negotiate with partners or others at home so that there is clarity about responsibilities, duties and tasks. Each person needs to have reasonable expectations of others and undertake a fair share of home responsibilities;
  - if you have problems or difficulties talk about them sooner rather than later at work and at home and get others to help in finding solutions;
  - if necessary think about the possibility of changing your pattern of work or hours of work or getting help in the home.

- Organisational culture

  - decide to what extent you want to or have to fit in. If the environment is competitive, do you want to compete? If you are ambitious and others are not, do you have to take on their norms? If it is a serious problem, for example racist or sexist, can you take action? Do you have to stay there?

- if the culture has poor communication systems find ways to communicate where you can;
- identify allies or like-minded people, form a group and work constructively towards changes you need or influence where you can;
- if you get no feedback, try asking managers or supervisors for feedback on your performance or for other information you need;
- identify people or mechanisms that can help you such as personnel or welfare staff, the trade union or other staff representatives so that they can help you communicate your needs or influence the culture;
- if all else fails, your organization may not be the place for you; try to find a new job as a positive move for you rather than through a sense of having failed to fit in or get on.

- Interpersonal relationships

  - no matter how difficult it seems you will have to start talking to people openly to resolve interpersonal relationship difficulties;
  - try to approach people positively, explaining how you feel and what you experience – avoid accusing;
  - have a proposal to put forward such as how you would like to work and relate to people;
  - seek other people's views and opinions and be prepared to listen to them and compromise;
  - try to agree a process for working towards better relationships that the two of you, or group, can review from time to time;
  - deal with interpersonal problems quickly; otherwise they generally get worse and not better. This may mean taking action (such as disciplinary action or bringing a grievance) that seems rather serious, but it can be a means of highlighting and dealing with the problem quickly while a solution is still possible;
  - if necessary consider outside help in resolving interpersonal relationship problems;
  - remember you do not have to make a personal friend of everyone you work with; agreeing mutually acceptable ways of working is often the best solution you will achieve.

9
Communication – Assertiveness

When faced with violence it is frequently very difficult to stop reacting long enough to think about and adopt the most appropriate behaviour in response. Often this is because of the shock or surprise and the emotional and biochemical reactions you are experiencing.

It is possible to learn different ways of behaving and to practise more 'positive' behaviour to a point where you can use it at will, even in difficult situations. One such more positive behaviour is assertive behaviour. Many people have found it helpful because it teaches them about themselves and their own 'usual' or 'habitual' behaviour patterns; it teaches them about a range of behaviour that they may experience from others and, on a practical level, it teaches strategies for managing interactions with others.

ASSERTIVE BEHAVIOUR

Assertive behaviour describes ways of relating to and interacting with other people that recognize and respect the rights, feelings, needs and opinions of both parties. It is an approach to communicating in which self-respect and respect for other people is demonstrated and it requires awareness and the taking of responsibility for oneself as well as enabling other people to do the same. Assertiveness is not about getting what you want all the time.

The concept of assertiveness is probably best understood by contrasting assertive behaviour with other types of behaviour such as aggressive behaviour, manipulative behaviour and behaviour that is variously described as passive, submissive or non-assertive, here described as passive.

Aggressive behaviour

Aggressive behaviour is characterized by

- recognizing one's own rights but not the rights of others;

- loud or forceful expressions of opinion;

- a need to prove superiority – to win whatever the cost;

- giving orders when a request would be more appropriate;

- personal criticism or attack, putting people down, picking on vulnerable points;

- belittling others' views, ideas and abilities;

- refusal to acknowledge other people's good points, contributions and so on;

- not listening to or considering others' opinions;

- competitiveness;

- failure to consider others' needs and priorities;

- making decisions regardless of others;

- verbal abuse, insults, rudeness;

- over-reacting;

- egocentricity, certainty of own importance;

- argumentativeness;

- creating conflict for its own sake;

- physical attack;

- wanting to be 'top dog' even at the expense of others;

- starting from the point of 'I'm important – you are not';

- behaving on the basis of 'I'm right – you are wrong';

- refusal to accept own mistakes and faults;

- threats, verbal or physical;

- 'I want' mentality, seeking always to meet own needs regardless of others;

- blaming others;

- interrupting people;

- being pushy, demanding.

Aggressive behaviour is not necessarily recognizable because someone is screaming and shouting or using aggressive language. Aggression can be conveyed quite clearly by body language even though the words used are not themselves aggressive, for example:

- tenseness of posture, facial expression;

- frowning, gritted teeth;

- narrowed, hard or staring eyes;

- sharp voice, too loud or strong in the situation;

- finger pointing or wagging;

- tapping of fingers or feet;

- trying to establish a higher physical position than others;

- getting too close – overbearing.

81

The effects of aggressive behaviour on other people can be:

- that they choose to alienate the aggressor for fear of attack;

- to leave them feeling hurt or humiliated;

- to provoke an aggressive response from them;

- to cause them to resent the aggressor;

- to leave them afraid to express opinions, ideas and so on;

- that they resort to indirect aggression, not retaliating but getting revenge in other ways;

- that they take in nothing that is said by the aggressor, dismissing it, finding no value in it because of the manner.

Despite appearances aggressive behaviour very often disguises a lack of self-esteem, self-confidence and self-awareness that leads to behaviour often described as win–lose behaviour. That is, an aggressor perceives the outcome of interactions with others as being one wins, one loses and they are hell bent on being the winner.

There are people who have naturally aggressive personalities, but generally people become aggressive in particular circumstances rather than as a rule. Examples of such circumstances are:

- under stress, when a loss of confidence can lead to people hiding their real feelings behind a show of aggression;

- following the example of others, people may adopt aggressive behaviour because they believe it will help them to succeed;

- because it works, aggressive behaviour that has succeeded in getting what someone wants may then be repeated;

- frustration with other people, bureaucracy or systems and so on can degenerate into aggression when other approaches do not work;

- anger that cannot be shown can be stored up and emerge as aggression;

- the culture of an organization can be aggressive so that people down the hierarchy experience aggressive approaches and repeat the behaviour;

- lack of skills in using assertive behaviour so people lapse into aggressive behaviour;

- anxiety leading to the desire to be in control and taking that control through aggressive behaviour (for example in a new job);

- where someone is forced into passive behaviour the resentment may build up and emerge as aggression – the worm turning!

Passive behaviour

Passive behaviour is characterized by:

- being the 'doormat' – people walk over you;

- failure to express own feelings, opinions and needs;

- difficulty in making decisions;

- letting others make decisions for you;

- making decisions without taking your own needs, wants and so on into account;

- perceiving self as a victim of others' unfairness, lack of consideration or circumstances;

- blaming someone or something else;

- putting self down – lack of self-respect, self-esteem;

- resignation – putting up with one's 'lot' in life;

- refusal to accept compliments;

- crying at any upset or threat;

- giving in, putting up with things;

- running away or avoiding any sort of confrontation;

- egocentricity from the point of always feeling 'done to';

- not knowing what you want;

- giving up at the first hurdle;

- waiting for others to guess what you want or need and provide it;

- not knowing where your own boundaries are – what is acceptable to you, what is enough;

- saying yes when you want to say no;

- allowing self to be pushed into things, interrupted, redirected;

- complaining behind the scenes rather than directly.

Passive behaviour does not normally include the person actually lying down like a doormat but much of the body language conveys their passivity or submissiveness quite clearly. The body language is particularly interesting in that almost opposite signs and signals convey it. For example:

• avoiding eye contact – deferential	• intense eye contact – taking in everything
• quiet, tentative, hesitant voice	• shrill, nervous voice
• nervous movements, agitation, fiddling, covering the mouth	• frozen, few or no gestures at all
• hunched or slumped posture, looking defeated	• tense or agitated posture – looking rigid
• looking defeated or tense	• pleading smiles, placating apologetic looks

The effects of passive behaviour on other people can be:

- that they feel annoyed and frustrated because they have to decide or do for the person;

- that they feel guilty about the 'victim';

- exasperation at the negative, whingeing approach;

- to trigger irritation that leads to aggression;

- that they isolate the passive or bullied person, being afraid to add to their burdens;

- to encourage them to make more and more demands of the passive or submissive person;

- that they fail to consider the passive person because their needs, views and so on are not made known or they simply appear to agree.

Passive (or submissive) behaviour generally stems from low self-esteem. It can become self-fulfilling in that the feedback from other people often confirms that the passive person is irritating, incompetent, indecisive and not worth bothering with.

Some people are habitually passive in their behaviour but, more commonly, there are reasons for passive behaviour being demonstrated, such as:

- gender conditioning that leads women to believe it is 'feminine' or 'right' to put others first in many circumstances;

- social conditioning that leads people to believe it is not 'nice' to seek to meet your own needs;

- frustration or bottled-up anger to a point where you just give up rather than blow up;

- stress or worry that leads to a loss of confidence or self-respect and so a failure to equate your own rights and needs with those of others;

- a desire to keep the peace or be liked so you give in rather than assert yourself;

- feeling threatened so you freeze or walk away from the situation or person;

- not knowing how to respond assertively, the only choice may be between uncharacteristic aggression or passive behaviour.

Manipulative behaviour

Manipulative behaviour is characterized by:

- never risking a direct approach, being fearful of rejection;

- covert expressions of views, ideas and feelings;

- skill at deceiving others;

- a need to be in control and manipulate others to avoid hurt or rejection;

- attacks on others that are disguised but usually well aimed;

- not trusting self or others;

- denial of feelings;

- wriggling out of situations – forgetting or making excuses rather than saying no;

- making others' decision for them but making sure they think they made the decision;

- appearing to take others into account but actually only paying lip service;

- insincerity, using compliments, flattery and flirting to get what you want;

- appearing to be one thing while signalling another;

- using rude remarks, derogatory body language, rather than being direct;

- making veiled threats, hinting at dangers or risks;

84

- obtrusiveness or dropping of hints – leading people to guess then blaming or resenting them for outcomes;

- using guilt as a weapon – backing people in to corners to get what is wanted;

- putting people down in a roundabout way so you appear to be caring or concerned;

- talking behind people's backs;

- sabotage behind the scenes.

Manipulative behaviour can often be accompanied by body language that is somewhat 'over the top'. There can be a tendency towards theatrics as if the person has created an image they are living up to rather than being themselves. Although on the surface overly friendly the body language can belie underlying aggression; for example:

- exaggerated or expansive gestures of friendliness, like slaps on the back, but the touching and patting may be patronizing;

- appearing to listen, be concerned and reacting but avoiding eye contact at crucial points, diverting attention from the speaker;

- sounding gentle, warm, pleading, friendly and so on but using underlying sarcasm, criticism, warnings or even threats;

- apparently relaxed posture, perhaps coy or flirtatious but sometimes making sure of physical dominance by being at a higher level than others;

- showing friendliness and closeness by being physically close to people but actually invading their space.

The effects of manipulative behaviour on other people can be:

- that they feel confused because of mixed messages;

- frustration because they cannot pin the manipulator down;

- guilt, because of 'guessing' wrongly or at allowing themselves to be manipulated;

- that they avoid manipulative people because they are too complicated;

- to retaliate by becoming aggressive or getting back at the manipulator by becoming manipulative themselves;

- that they will simply distrust the manipulative person in all situations, even if they are being genuine;

- hurt and/or anger because of feelings of being used.

Manipulative behaviour is indirectly aggressive. Manipulative people aim to get what they want but without being seen to want it. They also tend to have low self-esteem, being unable to be open about their needs, wants and feelings. They do not trust themselves to be straightforward and project that distrust on to others.

Some of the reasons why people may behave in a manipulative way are:

- it can be very effective in the short term in getting what they want or getting something done;

- manipulative behaviour breeds manipulative behaviour because no one trusts anyone so people cannot be open, honest or straightforward;

- the desire to be liked, to be seen as not demanding, can lead to trying to get what you want by roundabout means;

- stress or anxiety can lead to a need to be in control but not at any risk; manipulative behaviour allows you to pull the strings but deny responsibility if necessary;

- anger or frustration played out through manipulative behaviour rather than aggressive behaviour allows denial of any aggressive intent – the 'can't you take a joke' or the 'that wasn't what *I* had intended' approach;

- low self-confidence or self-esteem creates an inability to assert oneself.

Assertive behaviour

Assertive behaviour is characterized by:

- respect for self and self-esteem;

- respect for others;

- recognition of own and others' rights;

- acceptance of own positive and negative qualities and those of others;

- acknowledging own responsibility for own choices and actions;

- recognition of own needs, wants, feelings and the ability to express them and allowing others to do the same;

- listening to others;

- ability to ask for own needs to be met and risk refusal;

- accepting that one does not always get what one wants, feels rejection but is not destroyed by it;

- open and honest interaction with others;

- knowing own limits, can say 'no' and respecting others' limits or boundaries;

- giving feedback or constructive criticism when it is due, accepting it of yourself if valid or rejecting it if it is not.

Essentially assertive behaviour involves respecting yourself and your own rights while respecting others and their rights as well. It requires taking responsibility for yourself and allowing that others do the same for themselves. Assertive behaviour does not guarantee you will always get what you want. It is not about winning and losing but rather about 'win–win' situations where both parties are considered and treated as equal and the outcome is acceptable to both, even if one or other party does not get everything they wanted, because the reasons for it are understood.

Assertive behaviour is reflected in the words that are used but also by the non-verbal communication that accompanies it; for example:

- direct eye contact, but not peering or staring; showing attentiveness and listening;

- relaxed posture, normally well balanced, not fidgeting;

- facing people, but not threatening; rather giving them your attention;

- gestures in keeping with what is being said or felt, not agitated or nervous;

- open posture, without arms tightly folded or legs knotted around each other;

- firm, clear tone of voice but with appropriate expression of feeling;

- relaxed, open facial expression generally displaying appropriate reactions to what is said or feelings expressed.

The effects of assertive behaviour on other people can be:

- acceptance and ease of communication because the approach is straightforward;

- that they are less likely to misunderstand what is being said, asked for and so on;

- that they know where they stand with the assertive person so that insecurity is reduced;

- that they are less likely to respond non-assertively because of low levels of anxiety in the interaction;

- an inability to cope with an assertive approach because it is new to them.

Assertive behaviour is the most positive of the four approaches. Learning assertive behaviour can be helpful in a number of ways, for example:

- When faced with stressful situations an assertive approach helps you to deal with stress by boosting self-confidence and self-esteem as you consciously acknowledge your rights and needs in a situation.

- Assertiveness can help develop a balanced self-image, acknowledging your worth as a person, your abilities and qualities without becoming arrogant, while being able to recognize and accept faults and mistakes that you can then work on without punishing yourself.

- Assertiveness can help in controlling emotions such as anxiety because you can use learnt behaviour to prevent the emotions getting in the way but without denying them.

- If you feel frustration or anger assertive approaches will enable the appropriate expression of feelings rather than expressing them aggressively or bottling them up so that they become a problem later.

- Being assertive makes it easier for others to be assertive because it is a straightforward way of behaving.

- Demonstrating assertive behaviour can provide others with a model of effective behaviour that they can use.

- Using assertive behaviour in difficult situations can take courage and be stressful in the short term; however, the more you do it the easier it becomes.

- Assertive behaviour avoids you having the 'leftover' feelings associated with other sorts of behaviour, for example, guilt if you are agressive or manipulative, kicking yourself if you are passive and give in.

LEARNING TO BE ASSERTIVE

A first step in learning to be assertive is to be clear about your rights and those of other people.

You have the right:

- to state your needs, ask for what you want;

- to set your own priorities;

- to be treated with respect;

- to express your feelings, opinions and beliefs;

- to say yes or no for yourself;

- to be treated as an equal human being;

- to make mistakes;

- to change your mind;

- to say 'I don't undestand';

- to not seek approval;

- to decide for yourself;

- to decide whether or not you are responsible for solving others' problems.

It may seem unnecessary to list the rights people have but few of us consciously think about our rights at any time, let alone when we are in difficult situations, particularly if they involve aggressive behaviour towards us. For example, it is difficult to refuse to take responsibility for someone's problem when they are blaming you for it or when you are the representative of the organization they believe to have caused the problem. Similarly it takes quite an effort to confront a patronizing boss who treats you like a skivvy, even though you know you have a right to respect and to be treated as an equal human being.

Rights are not one-sided; just as you have these rights so does everyone else. As with all rights, these rights bring with them responsibilities: first, responsibility to ourselves to stand up for our rights and, second, the responsibility to respect the rights of others.

Like all skills assertiveness needs practice in the appropriate context; from the experience of that we can go on learning and developing the skills. It is not easy to learn to be assertive or to assert yourself in difficult situations but once you know the principles you just have to keep practising until it becomes second nature.

The following examples describe the assertive approach to the sort of interactions we all commonly have at work.

Making requests

- Before you can make requests assertively, it is necessary to know exactly what you want or need.

- In clarifying what it is you want or need you may have to stop thinking about what other people believe you ought to have or should have. Their expectations of you, or your perception of their expectations, can get in the way of you knowing what you want or need.

- This may sound selfish, probably because many of us are socialized out of expressing plainly our wants and needs in favour of what we ought to do or should do or doing the things that must be done.

- It is often easier to say what we don't want than what we do want. In the workplace one oftens hears 'Don't bother me with that now' as opposed to 'I want you to hang on to that until this afternoon's meeting and give it to me then'.

88

- Far from being selfish, clearly expressing your needs and wants helps the listener. It is a straightforward way of communicating that does not leave them guessing.

- If it is easier or more natural to start from the negative, do so. Decide what you don't want, work out the ideal alternative to that and what you will settle for, your fallback position, if the ideal is not on offer.

- Decide who you need to make the request to: this must be someone who can do something about it. Approaching or complaining to someone not involved or without the power to meet your request is a waste of time but a common feature of working life. One often hears people complaining to peers about their boss – 'I want him/her to listen to me' or 'I want him/her to tell me how I'm getting on' rather than saying it to the boss.

- When making a request to someone be sure you have their attention first. It is no good plucking up the courage if the other person is only half-listening or doing something else at the same time. Arrange a meeting time formally if you need to do that to ensure the other person's time and attention.

- When you make the request, do so clearly, concisely; say what you want or need positively and specifically; speak for yourself rather than generalizing and demonstrate appropriate strength of feeling through your tone of voice and body language.

- You don't have to go in with 'both feet' or 'all guns blazing'; that is much more likely to be, or appear, aggressive. Try starting off requests by saying, for example:

  'Will you please . . .?
  'Would you . . .?
  'Could you please . . .?
  'I'd like you to . . .?
  'I'd prefer you to . . .?

- If a request would seem to come out of the blue to someone, you may need to consider prefacing it with some feedback about what gives rise to it, for example: if you want your boss to tell you how you are getting on in your new job rather than carrying on trying to interpret her/his reactions you could try:

  'I like my new job very much but I don't feel I'm learning as much as I could or as quickly as I could. I'd like you to tell me what I do well, not so well, things you'd like me to do differently.'

- There is a wide range of possible responses to requests, from agreement to direct refusal; some of them will be more difficult to deal with than others. If you get an unsatisfactory response you will need to decide if your request is important enough to persist with.

- Sticking to your request is one form of persistence and you should repeat it, perhaps in slightly different but no less clear ways, until it is heard, understood and taken seriously.

- Reflecting the response you get and sticking to your request is another way of persisting, so:
  - pay attention to the other person's response;
  - respond to relevant questions – ignore irrelevant ones that would divert you;
  - summarize what the other person has said very briefly;
  - make your request again.

89

- If you do persist in your request you must keep your tone of voice and body language relaxed and calm. You don't want the exchange to become aggressive.

- Persistence is fine until it becomes clear that to persist further would mean failing to respect the other person's rights, needs and wants. At this point you may need to accept you cannot have the ideal and try to achieve your previously identified 'fallback position' as part of a compromise.

Expressing opinions

One of your rights described earlier is the right to hold an opinion and have it heard. When expressing opinions assertively try to remember:

- You may need to create the opportunity to express your opinion by
    - arranging to meet someone to put your opinion forward;
    - interrupting if the other person does not give you a chance to speak otherwise;
    - writing to someone.

- In expressing yourself you should make a clear, concise statement of your opinion. Speak for yourself; say 'I think', 'I believe', 'in my opinion', 'it seems to me' rather than generalizing or dressing up your opinion as fact.

- Other people also have the right to their opinions and to have them heard, so give others the chance to speak without interrupting, as far as possible; listen to them, do not belittle their views and respect their right to a different opinion from yours.

- If someone tries to interrupt you continuously you can either ignore it and continue or say something like 'let me finish . . .' or 'hold on, I have not finished yet . . .'. When you have finished you can then ask them what they were going to say and listen to them.

- There are times when it is best to agree to disagree and leave it at that.

- Finding the common ground is a very positive step towards reaching agreement. Try to identify where you do agree and work from that positive point.

- Non-verbal communication is just as important as what you say; avoid adopting a posture or tone of voice that could be construed as aggressive especially when expressing opposing views.

Discussion

Discussion is a feature of many kinds of activities in the workplace. We all know how many meetings we have to attend! Discussion can serve all sorts of purposes such as generating ideas, making decisions, canvassing opinions, testing out ideas, resolving problems, creating proposals and plans or building relationships. Everyone involved in the discussion should have something to contribute, otherwise they should not be there. Thus it follows that everyone should have an equal opportunity to join in fully.

However, discussions are often inbalanced, for example, with one or more people doing most of the talking and others doing the listening. This can leave the talkers feeling the listeners are not contributing and are selfishly keeping ideas and opinions safely to themselves while the talkers are sharing and taking the risks. The listeners, on the other hand, may well feel they are being taken for granted, not being noticed or that people are not interested in them or their views. An assertive approach to discussion, whatever its purpose, can help you as an individual as well as the process of the discussion, thereby making it more effective from everyone's perspective.

The following are suggestions as to how you could take an assertive approach to discussions.

- While you would normally intervene in the conversation at an appropriate point you may find that if you cannot get a word in you need to create space for yourself by interrupting. If someone is in full flow it may be hard to attract attention away from what they are saying. Try using a phrase that gives the speaker a chance to switch their attention to you and makes it clear you want to contribute, such as:

  'I'd like to comment on that . . .'
  'I want to make a point here . . .'
  'May I just add . . .'
  'Before we lose the point . . .'

- If you need to interrupt use body language as well to demonstrate that there is no aggression on your part; you just want to speak. Appropriate body language can also help defuse any defensive aggression from the person interrupted.

- When you are speaking do not allow people to interrupt you until you have had a reasonable time to have your say. Stick to your point, say 'let me finish'. Demonstrate by body language too that you don't want to take over but just want an equal chance to put your point across.

- Acknowledge that there may be times when you go on too long and other people will interrupt you for that reason; you must respect their right to a say as well.

- Give other people the chance to respond to what you have said.

- If people are not acknowledging what you have said or responding to it, try asking open questions such as 'How do you see it?', 'What do you think?' or 'What were you going to say?'.

- In some discussions you may have to persist in breaking into the conversation in order to assert your right to equal opportunity of expression. Most people eventually get the message that you want to take an equal part in the proceedings.

- If people do not get the message that you want to contribute on an equal basis with others you may have to raise it as a problem. Don't blame people; simply say how you feel and what you want people to do differently.

- Should you find yourself doing most of the talking you may have to stay deliberately quiet at times and/or invite other people to speak by asking questions or seeking a view from them.

- If you are doing most of the talking it may be that you need to practise listening skills. One way is to listen to the speaker, picking out the key points of what they are saying so that at the end you can summarize what they have said.

- Observe body language so that you know when to stop talking: people fiddling or doodling, slumped in their chairs or gazing out the window may well be telling you they have listened enough.

- Behaviour in a group can sometimes be unacceptable to some or all of the members, for example, racist or sexist language, mocking someone, swearing or outright aggres-

91

sion towards a group member. An assertive approach to handling such a situation would be

– not to accuse or blame
– to own the problem and explain, for example, 'I am upset by that sort of language because . . .' or 'I feel really put down when you say . . .', followed by a clear statement of what you want, an assertive request: 'I'd prefer you not to . . .' or 'would you stop . . .'

Saying 'No'

Saying 'yes' when you really mean or want to say 'no' can leave you feeling exploited or 'put upon'. You may end up resenting other people and getting angry with yourself because you are expending time and energy on others' priorities rather than your own. Responding to everyone else's requests can give you a short-term feeling of being helpful, cooperative and supportive but you may find you get little job satisfaction from doing others' tasks and have little time to devote to your own job and developing yourself in it. Eventually the standard of your work may be affected because you take on too much and that, combined with resentment of yourself and others, can result in depression. Being a martyr can ultimately bring out the worst in the nicest people.

Saying no can be difficult and stressful at the start but it gets easier with practice and offsets the longer-term risks of not doing so. Saying no assertively involves:

* knowing what you want to do rather than what you 'ought' or 'should' do;

* having all the information you need, or obtaining it, before you make a decision;

* bearing in mind that turning down a request is just that, not rejecting the person;

* making a clear, concise statement, preferably including the word 'no' when you turn down a request – try 'No, I'm not willing to . . .' or 'I'm not prepared to, no . . .';

* persisting in the refusal if you really do not want to comply;

* saying 'no' and leaving it at that in some situations such as when people try to manipulate you or goad you into argument;

* giving your reasons for saying 'no' if appropriate, polite or humane to do so, but do keep them short and to the point;

* giving your reasons once; there is no need to repeat them or justify them, especially where clever manipulative or aggressive people will try to invalidate them;

* not feeling you have to give reasons if the other person is not entitled to them or they are personal;

* apologizing only when it is genuine or polite; if you continually apologize it will appear insincere or you may slide into submissive behaviour;

* suggesting alternatives if appropriate; for example, you may be willing to comply with the request at another time or may know someone who would be interested in doing so;

* showing concern about the feelings of the person whose request you are refusing by saying you do not intend to hurt their feelings or reject them. The concern really must be genuine if it is to be assertive or of any value;

92

- sometimes feeling guilty or mean because you think people may not cope with your refusal or that their needs or wants should come before your own;

- remembering that some people will be annoyed, offended or hurt by a refusal and others will not; the majority of people are nonetheless quite able to cope;

- remembering you are important too and have the right to decide your own priorities.

Negotiation

Assertiveness is sometimes about refusing requests, saying 'no' and thus not cooperating. Assertiveness can also mean total cooperation if appropriate and, between the two extremes, there is negotiation and compromise. Negotiation and compromise are commonly needed in many workplaces in all kinds of circumstances, from sorting out some interpersonal 'tiff' to major management and union negotiations. Assertive negotiation involves:

- deciding on your ideal preference in the situation and how strongly you feel about achieving it;

- deciding a 'fallback position', a second order preference that you will settle for;

- communicating your ideal preference and the strength of your feeling about it to the other person/s;

- finding out the ideal preference of the other party and their strength of feeling about it;

- taking into acocunt the preferences and feelings of both sides, decide if/when it is appropriate to reveal your second preference;

- finding out what the other party is willing to settle for. If you have not done so already, reveal your second preference;

- establishing agreement with the other party if at all possible;

- sticking to your guns about your second preference if the other party tries to push you beyond that;

- being prepared for give and take in the process but knowing what your boundaries are and communicating them clearly;

- accepting that not every negotiation will achieve the ideal win–win result where everyone feels that they have achieved something, and that they agree to and are committed to the outcome.

Feedback

Feedback is a way of giving people information about how they affect us or obtaining information about how we affect others. Skilful feedback is a helpful, enabling, learning process whether it is critical or complimentary.

Giving and receiving feedback is a form of assertive communication but it does not always come easily to us. People are often not good at giving or receiving compliments or constructive criticism, partly through a lack of skills and practice and partly through fear of hurting or embarrassing themselves or others.

93

Some general guidelines for giving feedback

- Start with the positive. When offering feedback it can help the receiver to hear first what you like, appreciate, enjoy or what you feel they did well.

  We can easily slip into emphasizing the negative, the focus being on mistakes rather than strengths and in the rush to criticize the positive aspects are overlooked. If the positive is registered first the negative is more likely to be listened to and acted upon.

- Be specific. General comments, hints or suggestions are not very helpful because they leave the listener guessing. Comments such as 'that was fine', 'you were terrible' or 'you did OK' rarely tell the listener what it was they did well or not well. It is difficult for the listener to act on general, overall comments.

- Be descriptive rather than evaluative. Describe your reactions by telling the person what you saw or heard and the effect it had on you. Simply commenting on something as 'good' or 'bad', 'wrong' or 'right' is not informative and such value judgements can lead to defensiveness, for example: 'I feel you were really interested and concerned because of the way you leant forward, nodded and said enough to signal that you were listening carefully' is much more helpful than 'that was fine, you did well'.

- Only give feedback on what can be changed. Giving feedback to someone about something over which they have little or no control or choice is not only unhelpful; it is pointless and can create frustration and resentment.

  'Your bushy eyebrows make you look aggressive' is not offering information about which the listener can do very much and could well hurt or antagonize them, making constructive feedback between you impossible.

  Information such as 'I think it would help if you smiled a bit more and tried to avoid frowning when you are thinking hard' gives the listener ideas that they can choose to work on if they wish.

- Time it carefully. Feedback is often most useful as early as possible after the behaviour so that events and feelings are remembered. However, it is important to be as sure as possible that the receiver is ready for the feedback at that stage; in some situations it may be more helpful to reserve feedback until later.

- Offer alternatives. In situations where you offer negative feedback, suggesting what could have been done differently is often more helpful than simply criticizing. Turn the negative feedback into a positive suggestion such as 'I know everyone was eager to get on with the business when I brought the new manager in today, but you did seem unwelcoming; perhaps next time we can stop for a moment to introduce everyone properly'.

- Check out. Don't assume the feedback you give is immediately understood or that the message received was the message intended. Check out with the other person to ensure understanding.

- Own the feedback. Start with 'I': 'I feel annoyed, 'I was pleased' or 'In my opinion', rather than dressing up your views, feelings and opinions as facts. All you can honestly offer the other person is your experience of them at a particular time and it is very important to take responsibility for the feedback you offer.

- Don't overdo it. When asked for comments and opinions it is tempting to say everything and overwhelm the receiver. It is more effective to select the most appropriate and useful information, leaving the receiver to ask for more if they wish.

- Leave the receiver a choice. Feedback which demands change or tries to impose it on the receiver invites resistance and may lead to aggression. Feedback is not about telling people what they must do but what is preferable from the giver's point of view.

- Questions first. Posing questions can help the receiver to start assessing or analysing their own behaviour and enable you to give feedback they will perceive as relevant and helpful.

- Be objective. Offering facts before opinions and describing observable behaviour helps to avoid total subjectivity. It can also help put observations into context and give the listener information about the behaviour as well as its effects on you from your perspective.

Giving critical feedback

- Even well-intended, constructive criticism won't make you popular; you need to decide what is important: being liked or getting the message across.

- If criticism is due it may be kinder sooner rather than later, thus offering the receiver the chance to do something about it now – criticism should be given in private, preferably face-to-face and make sure there is enough time to discuss it.

- Be clear about what you prefer the listener to do.

- Make sure the listener understands the positive and negative consequences of acting or not acting on the criticism.

- If you are uncomfortable or awkward about criticizing you can say so, for example, 'It's difficult for me to say this, but I think you should know . . .' or 'I'm concerned about upsetting you but I feel I must tell you . . . because . . .'

- You may need to persist with the feedback if you meet resistance and you really feel it is essential to get the point over.

- End on a positive note: thank the receiver for listening, set the criticism in the context of what they do well.

Giving complimentary feedback

- It may seem a bit 'soppy' when you come to say something complimentary that you have been thinking, but do say it. More expressions of appreciation would help the atmosphere of many workplaces.

- Make sure the compliment is genuine and for its own sake, not to achieve other ends.

- Avoid making a song and dance of it as this may simply embarrass the receiver or appear insincere.

- Let them know exactly what they did well or what was appreciated so that it can be repeated.

- Compliments do not have to be flowery and effusive; a simple 'thank you' for something or 'well done' in relation to a piece of work is generally adequate.

Receiving feedback

- Listening. Feedback can be uncomfortable to hear sometimes but it is better than not knowing what others think and feel. Listen to the feedback because it may help you; you will remain entitled to ignore it if you decide it is irrelevant, insignificant or about behaviour you wish to maintain for other reasons.

- Be sure you understand. Make sure you understand what the giver of feedback is saying before you respond. Avoid jumping to conclusions, becoming defensive or going on the attack as all these will deter people from giving you feedback. Check you have understood by asking questions or by paraphrasing what you believe was said.

- Check with others. If you rely on only one source of information, you may get a very individual or a biased view. Ask other people for feedback as you may find they experience you differently. The more information you have, the more likely you are to develop a balanced view of yourself and keep feedback in perspective.

- Ask for feedback. If you do not get feedback you may need to ask for it. Obtaining feedback is much more useful than trying to guess what people think or feel, how others perceive you, your performance and so on. You may need to help people unused to giving feedback to provide you with information that is useful to you. You may also have to cope with people not able to give feedback very skilfully.

- Don't waste it. Knowing how other people experience us helps develop self-awareness; otherwise we have only our own perceptions of ourselves to go by. Feedback can be a useful contribution to self-development, provided that it is used.

- Acting on feedback. Having received feedback you need to consider how accurate and valuable you believe it is and the consequences of acting or not acting on it. You can then make your choice.

- Thank the giver. Saying thank you, apart from being polite, acknowledges that the person who gave you feedback may have found it very difficult to do and you may benefit greatly from it. Thanking the giver also reinforces the positive practice of giving feedback that is valuable in any relationship or organization.

Receiving complimentary feedback

- Accepting compliments can be difficult but, like gifts, if they are not accepted the giver may feel hurt, rejected or humiliated and is unlikely to try to give again.

- Compliments should be accepted without embarrassment. It sometimes takes practice to simply say 'thank you' or 'it is kind of you to say so', 'it's nice to be appreciated'. You can always say 'I'm a little embarrassed but thank you'; that way people know why you are reacting as you are but that you do not want them to avoid complimenting you.

- It is not immodest to accept compliments when they are due.

- Avoid dismissing compliments with phrases such as 'I'm not really' or 'It was nothing'; it puts people off positive feedback and if you later want positive feedback and do not get it you may blame yourself.

- Avoid denying your own skill, expertise or achievement. By trying to give the credit to others you may make the giver feel foolish and you may regret it one day.

- Resist responding to a compliment with 'but not as well as you' or 'you would have done it better'. The giver may believe you think they are insincere in their compliment.

- Allow the giver the pleasure of giving.

- If you believe the giver of the compliment has an ulterior motive accept the compliment and deal with the hidden agenda at a separate time.

Receiving critical feedback

- Constructive, well-timed and supportive criticism can still make you feel awful, especially if you have been on the receiving end of damaging criticism in the past. On the other hand it can be very beneficial.

- There is nothing worse than discovering too late you could have done better or differently (the 'I wish I'd known' syndrome).

96

- Decide how much truth there is in the criticism offered: do you agree entirely, in part or totally disagree?

- Accept valid criticism without being defensive, justifying yourself, excusing or passing the buck.

- If you do not accept the criticism you can reject it without rejecting the other person: say you 'disagree' but not 'you are wrong'. The latter is a confrontational response, inviting the other person to prove the opposite.

- If you partly agree be clear about that part you agree with and what you disagree with.

- If the giver of criticism makes generalizations such as 'you always do . . .' you can find out exactly what they are getting at by explaining you are unclear and asking questions, for example 'what exactly did I do or say . . .?', 'can you give me an example of . . .?', 'can you describe what it is that . . .?'. In this way you can pinpoint your behaviour that gave rise to the critcism and help identify the emotional effects of your actions on others. If you explain that you need more information and ask questions in a way that is not defensive, challenging or aggressive you can obtain the necessary information to decide whether you agree or not with the criticism.

- Another aspect of questions is that they can help demonstrate when criticism is unfair or vindictive because the giver is unlikely to be able to provide the information, examples, descriptions and so on to support the criticism. In view of this you can clearly state that you disagree; the process may put the person off future unfair or vindictive criticism.

- When the criticism is intended to be or proves to be helpful to you thank the giver; it may have been difficult for them to give and constructive criticism is a practice that should be encouraged.

Workwise – Good Practice Guide

This chapter contains a series of guidelines on good practice for different areas and different types of work.

TRAVELLING

Many people do not work solely in the workplace; their job requires them to travel on foot, public transport or in a private car. Although we should all feel free to come and go, and do our jobs as required, there are inevitably risks involved in travelling.

Employers need to remember that employees travelling on business are still their responsibility and should consider developing written guidelines and procedures for staff.

It is sometimes difficult for employers to implement recording processes so that it is known where staff are, with whom, when they are expected back and so on because:

- employees don't like having 'tabs kept on them';

- employees feel they are not trusted and need to be checked up on;

- things change and arrangements are altered so it is difficult to remember to amend records;

- if employers create a procedure then it needs to be monitored and some sanctions available if it is not adhered to, and of course this means more work.

The need to know where people are may have to be 'sold' to employees. To do this they will need to be shown the risks of working alone, being isolated, not being contactable and not being missed.

Selling the idea could including providing evidence of what has actually happened to people using examples from their own workplace of situations where people have been 'missing' or out of touch. It is far better to persuade employees that such recording is needed but, if all else fails, an employer may have to insist it is done unilaterally.

How the recording is implemented will depend on the particular workplace and work patterns. Before you establish a system make the 'rules' clear, for example:

- no one must ever visit any client or contact without checking they are genuine;

- no one should give out private telephone numbers;

- everyone must complete a recording form regardless of the length or type of visit or if it involved another person.

Some examples of recording systems that work for organizations follow.

1. A book is kept at the reception desk of the office building and *everyone* signs in and out. When they sign out they note where they are going, with whom or whom they are meeting, when they are expected back and how they can be contacted (telephone number). The receptionist is responsible for raising the alarm if the person does not return within an hour of the time they were expected and the person's manager is then responsible for attempting to make contact.

2. Every member of staff has a desk diary provided by the organization and they are required to fill it in with all details of visits, meetings and so on outside the office. Individuals are responsible for keeping the diary correct, if necessary telephoning in changes to secretaries or administrative staff.

3. Each team of staff has a team administrator who is assigned the responsibility for providing a weekly diary sheet which he/she keeps. Staff are responsible for notifying the administrator of any changes or any delays in returning. If staff do not return when expected the administrator notifies the team leader who then attempts to make contact.

A general warning about the giving of personal telephone numbers should be given to all travelling staff or those who work away from their base. There is often a temptation for staff who are often out of the office or who are travelling to give their home telephone numbers and/or addresses to clients, contacts or customers. This is unwise practice except in particular circumstances where the person is very well known to, or a friend of, the employee.

If it really is necessary for the employee to be contactable outside working hours the provision of a mobile 'phone, a pager or a special work 'phone line should be considered.

Travelling on foot

Travelling on foot is often the easiest and quickest way of getting around, especially in a town or city. It is generally a safe means of travel but the risks increase, of course, when it is dark as it is on winter afternoons.

The following guidelines provide advice on keeping safe on foot:

- Think ahead, be alert and aware of your surroundings.

- Try to avoid walking alone at night.

- Keep to busy, well lit roads.

- Do not take short cuts.

- Avoid poorly lit or quiet underpasses.

- Walk facing oncoming traffic to avoid kerb crawlers.

- If you have to walk in the same direction as the traffic and a driver stops simply turn and walk the other way; the driver cannot follow.

99

- If a driver stops write down the registration number; the driver will almost certainly leave immediately.

- If you think you are being followed cross the road and keep walking. If you are still being followed make for the nearest busy area, open shop, well lit house and so on and ask for help if necessary.

- Do not wait around unless you absolutely must. If you must, keep to lighted or busy areas and look confident and positive.

- Never accept lifts unless you know and trust the driver and never hitch lifts.

- If you carry money or valuables use a money belt.

- Keep your hands free to defend yourself.

- Carry an alarm, but in your hand so you can use it, not in a handbag or briefcase.

- Avoid areas where you know groups hang about, for example, pubs and clubs.

- Don't switch off to the world by wearing a personal radio or stereo.

Using Cabs

In London, Hackney carriages (black taxis) are licensed by the Police. Each cab has a white plate with black lettering, giving the licence number. The plate is inside the cab and on the outside. The driver must wear a badge in a conspicuous place. Mini-cabs or private hire vehicles are unlicensed. However, most mini-cab drivers are reliable and honest, but like all professions, they have their bad apples.

- Make sure you have the 'phone number of a reputable cab company. Ask your friends for a recommendation.

- When you book your cab ask the company for the driver's name and call sign. Ask what type of car is being used.

- If you are calling from a public place, try to avoid doing so where someone overhears you giving your name and so on. Anyone could pull up and call 'cab for Mary Smith' so when your cab arrives, check the driver's name and confirm the company name.

- If you can share a cab with a friend, so much the better; it's cheaper too.

- Whilst you may not wish to appear unfriendly, always sit in the back.

- If you do chat with the driver don't give any personal details away.

- If you feel uneasy with the driver ask to stop at a busy familiar place and get out.

- Before you arrive at your destination have your cash ready, leave the cab and pay the driver.

- Have your door keys ready and enter your home quickly.

Beware of bogus mini-cabs! Some people do not work for mini-cab firms at all. They put an aerial on the roof of their car and have a pretend handset. They unlawfully ply for hire at busy night spots. They gain fares by calling out 'Someone ordered a cab?' On a busy night with a shortage of transport it could be tempting, but it is much safer to wait.

Using Private Cars

Whether the car you are using is your own vehicle, leased through your company, hired or provided by your company the following guidelines apply.

- Keep your car in good working order, have it serviced regularly and check it regularly.

- If you hire a car ensure it has been checked or check it yourself.

- Carry extra petrol in a safety-approved portable petrol tank.

- Be a member of one of the breakdown/rescue organizations; employers often pay for this if you are required to use your car on business or it is part of the package when you lease a car or have a company car.

- Consider a car 'phone if you travel a lot; in some cases an employer may provide or contribute to this.

- Make sure you have change and a 'phone card for use in an emergency.

- Always have the necessary maps and directions in the car so you do not have to stop to ask.

- Stay in the car as much as possible. Keep the doors locked and windows closed when you can, especially in towns when you must stop at lights, junctions, and so on.

- Keep handbags, briefcases and so on out of reach of open windows in case of snatch thieves.

- When leaving the car always lock equipment, luggage, valuables and so on in the boot. Leave nothing on display.

- Lock your car, even if you only go to pay for petrol on a garage forecourt.

- When you park in daylight consider what the area will be like in the dark.

- At night, park in a well lit place and one that is busy, if possible. Avoid multi-storey car parks or car parks where you and your vehicle are not clearly visible.

- Before you get in the car check the back seat: keep a torch for the purpose.

- If you see an incident or accident or someone tries to flag you down *don't* stop to investigate without thinking – is it safe? Could you help? Would it be safer and more use if you went for help?

- If a car pulls up in front of you and you have to stop, keep the engine running; if you turn if off and then try to restart it in a hurry you may flood it.

- If you think you are being followed try to alert other drivers – use the lights and horn. Keep driving until you reach a busy area or a police, fire or ambulance station or a garage.

- If anyone approaches you in your car when you are stationary stay in the car with the doors locked and the windows closed. If the engine is running, keep it running. If not, start the car. If you are in any doubt at all drive off; if you can't, make as much noise and fuss as possible.

- Any attempt to force entry into your car such as someone trying to force down a partially open window may need to be met with force. Use your alarm if it is to hand but also consider de-icer spray, fire extinguisher, the heel of your shoe, cigar lighter. If you can surprise the attacker the advantage is yours and you can get away.

101

- Avoid taking people (clients, customers, contacts) in your car on your own unless they are friends or very well known to you.

Motorways

Travel on motorways is of concern, especially when a breakdown occurs or assistance is needed. There is a debate on whether to remain in a car and put up a HELP sign in the back window or to walk to the telephone and, having made the call, should you stay in the car or stand on the bank?

- If you can safely drive to an emergency telephone then do so, stopping with the front passenger door of the car level with the telephone as far to the left as possible.

- Switch on your hazard lights; if leaving the vehicle do so by the nearside door. Leave any animals in the car.

- Never cross the carriageway to reach a closer telephone and never reverse your car to a telephone.

- If you cannot drive further, a marker post (every 100 metres) will point to the nearest 'phone. 'Phones are set 1000 metres apart, so you will never need to walk further than 500 metres. No money is required: as soon as you lift the handset, it will start ringing in the Police control room. You do not need to say where you are; they will know.

- Stand behind the 'phone, facing oncoming traffic, so you can see if anyone approaches you. The passing traffic makes it very noisy so you may have to shout.

- Tell the control if you are a woman on your own. They will covertly alert a police car to check you are ok if at all possible. On some urban motorways they may be able to see you on closed circuit television.

- If your car is not near the 'phone then note the numbers on the nearest marker post. Tell the control room the problem, having your breakdown organization card and your registration number ready.

Stay in your car or stand on the verge?

The Highway Code section 173 advises *you* to decide whether or not to stay in the car or leave it and stand on the verge. However, 10 per cent of all fatal motorway accidents take place when a vehicle collides with a stationary car parked on the hard shoulder. In 1988, 25 such fatal accidents occurred in this way.

The issue of the use of a HELP LONE WOMAN sign placed in the car rear window is not straightforward. Apart from a police patrol not passing by for some time (due to accidents elsewhere) it may advertise the fact that you are alone. If a genuine good Samaritan then stops to help, are you going to get out of the vehicle or refuse to do so? Should you open the window to speak?

If you are alone and decide to stay in the vehicle, whether you have 'phoned the police first or not, sit in the nearside seat: it gives the impression that there is someone with you nearby. Keep all doors locked and windows closed. If you decide to stay in the car remember that it could be involved in an accident.

If you decide to stand on the verge, try to stay out of sight of passing cars. Lock all car doors but leave the passenger door fully open so that you can get back in quickly if you decide to. Then lock the passenger door behind you. Do not leave the keys in the car.

If you are by the 'phone and someone stops, use the 'phone to tell the police and give them the registration number of the car that has stopped.

102

When the breakdown truck arrives check that he/she knows your name and has in fact been sent to you. Some breakdowns cruise waiting to pirate custom.

Crime prevention advantages must be weighed against remaining in a vehicle in a potentially hostile environment.

The advice from the Department of Transport, Police, RAC and AA is to stay on the verge, only re-entering the car if you feel in danger; try to decide by taking all the factors into consideration: the weather (fog, rain, snow, sunshine), the time of day and whether it is a dark, deserted country stretch or a busy well lit urban area.

Public Transport

Public transport here includes buses, trains and underground services.

- Always sit near the bus driver on a 'one-man bus' or stay downstairs on a double decker bus with a conductor.

- Wait for the bus, if possible, at a busy stop that is well lit or a bus stop close to areas of activity, for example, a garage or a late shop.

- Have your fare ready in your hand or pocket, separate from other money or valuables.

- Try to avoid having your hands full with heavy bags.

- Wear sensible shoes in case you need to run; be ready to kick off other shoes if necessary.

- On trains single enclosed compartments are now fairly rare but when you see them, avoid them. Sit in an open compartment near the alarm pull if you can or at least register where it is.

- If there is a guard on the train sit in the nearest compartment to the guard.

- In stations note where the exits are so you can leave readily.

- Don't doze off: stay alert to what is going on around you.

- If you do not like the look of someone change carriages.

- In underground stations, keep your eyes open and note the exits and station alarm panel.

- On tube trains sit in busy compartments.

- Carry a personal alarm in your hand – it is no use in a bag.

- Avoid travelling alone late at night on any form of public transport if at all possible.

Staying in hotels

- Park nearby if possible in a well lit area where you and your vehicle can easily be seen.

- At reception avoid other people overhearing your name and room number.

- Avoid rooms that are accessible from outside, for example on the ground floor, or with a fire escape outside.

- If there is a safety chain on the door or a lock preventing access with a pass key, use it.

- Use a door alarm if you have one.

- Never go to other people's rooms unless you are absolutely sure you are safe.

- Never invite people to your room unless you know you are safe.

- If you hear any disturbance stay in your room and call for help.

- Do not wander around hotel grounds after dark.

- If you feel safer avoiding the dining room order your meal in your room.

RECEPTION AREAS/WAITING ROOMS

Reception areas and waiting areas are very often the public face of an organization for most outsiders. They are also the area where the majority of people will start their contact with the organization.

The environment and service in reception and waiting areas may not particularly affect visitors who simply come to attend a meeting, but if someone has come to sort out a disagreement, deal with a problem, make a complaint or is there other than by choice the effect could be quite significant.

There is evidence from research to show that colour can affect mood and perception. Dark, dingy places feel different from bright, welcoming, warm ones. Institutional colours, such as grey and greens, can lead to certain perceptions of places or confirm our preconceived ideas of what places (and possible the people in them too) are like. Being left to wait in a dark, dingy, cold or grubby room is unlikely to improve anyone's mood. It has also been shown that smells can create unease, especially those that are evocative of potentially uncomfortable situations such as hospitals or dentists. A bright, warm, comfortable setting will not guarantee good humour but it can be calming rather than irritating.

Just as the environment can affect people coming into it as visitors, it can also affect people who work there, even to the point of predisposing them to behaviour that may elicit an aggressive response.

A number of organizations have taken this research seriously and applied it to reception and waiting areas in the following ways:

- using pastel colours;

- putting flowers or plants in waiting areas;

- using light and airy rooms for waiting;

- providing comfortable seating;

- making reading material available;

- providing play areas and/or toys for children;

- playing background music or providing TV;

- putting in drinks machines or otherwise making refreshments available;

104

- ensuring there are toilet and baby changing facilities;

- installing a telephone so people waiting feel they can still communicate with the world outside;

- avoiding stressful noise such as loud music, irritating public address systems or machine noise;

- making sure there is adequate and accessible parking so people do not arrive frustrated;

- providing directions, maps, details of money required in car parks and so on so people can come prepared.

Organizations that take these sorts of steps believe they are cost-effective and make a difference because:

- difficulty in finding the place, parking and so on is minimized and so is frustration;

- people feel welcome and expected;

- it appears that the organization has respect for visitors and concern for their comfort;

- people are less likely to feel anonymous, like a number waiting in line;

- waiting is relatively pleasurable so people do not become increasingly uncomfortable, tense and irritated;

- providing books, reading material, refreshments and so on creates diversion and interest and avoids boredom.

Many people report that the thing most guaranteed to 'wind them up' while waiting is not knowing what is going on or how long they will be expected to wait.

Some organizations use a ticket system and a display that shows the progress through the queue of people waiting. People may not entirely like the number approach but it does help to indicate how close they are to being seen.

Other organizations train receptionists to give callers an estimated waiting time. However, this can backfire if the time is then not adhered to.

Another approach is for reception staff to go into waiting areas from time to time with a list of the people waiting and give them a 'status report': For example, 'there are three people to be seen before you'; 'Mrs X has one person with her, then she'll see you'. Again this can backfire if one person takes much longer than was expected but at least people are being given information and receptionists can update information from time to time.

Perhaps the most straightforward way of managing waiting time is to arrange appointments whenever possible. It is essential to allow a realistic time for each appointment if such a system is to work; otherwise a queue will build up and people may be even more annoyed because they were on time for their appointments.

Reception staff themselves can be in very vulnerable positions, especially where public access means anyone can walk into the organization.

Some examples of good practice in organization reception areas include:

- using wider counters so staff cannot be reached across them;

- raising the height of the floor on the staff side of counters, again to protect them from people reaching over;

- using protective screens;

- providing a panic button or other alarm system;

105

- providing security cameras so reception staff can see all areas from a safe position;

- reorganizing office layout so reception staff are visible to other staff;

- making sure reception staff have an escape route should they need it;

- providing entry 'phone/entry camera systems in organizations with limited access;

- locking access to counter-protected reception areas;

- one-way doors to reception areas;

- receptionists are notified by other employees of all expected visitors; other callers such as deliveries, tradespeople or contractors can use a visitor form;

- intercom links with back up from nominated staff – or people can listen in if they see worrying behaviour.

Many of the safety and security devices have proved necessary and successful in organizations. However, it ought to be remembered that what is meant as protection for staff can seem like a barrier to the client or customer. Counters, screens and other devices can trigger aggression or violence in some people when they are perceived as a barrier or block.

A balance needs to be achieved between creating a welcoming, calming, unthreatening environment for clients and customers while ensuring the safety of staff. Where that balance lies in any given organization will need to be worked out.

ACCESS TO THE WORKPLACE

Access to the workplace very often centres around the main door and reception service. Certainly this area is important but there are relatively few organizations with one entrance controlled by a reception service.

Most have back doors, fire doors, service bays, car park entrances and so on. All these are potential points of access into the building and may well be preferred points of access for anyone with villainy in mind!

Even where there is general public access to a building it is possible to confine that access to public areas so that employees come to the public rather than find members of the public wandering around the building. Limiting access can be achieved by using:

- locked doors that can be operated by a key, key card or access number punched in by staff;

- one-way doors. These can be used by staff to exit at any time and meet fire regulations but entry can only be effected by use of a key system. If these doors are used as an escape route for staff other doors may also be needed in case they could not use the key system in an emergency;

- offices off the reception or waiting area where employees can meet members of the public but can be seen by and see reception and/or security staff.

Access to buildings (where there is not general public access) or to parts of buildings can also be controlled if

- all visitors and other callers are notified to reception or security so they are expected;

- visitors and/or tradespersons use the entrance marked;
- visitors sign in and out so it is known who is in the building and when they leave;
- all legitimate visitors wear a pass or visitor's badge;
- all visitors are met by an employee and remain their responsibility throughout the visit;
- 'no entry' signs can be used;
- there are 'staff only' notices posted;
- even staff wear badges in big organizations so they are seen as staff;
- there is a reception or security area on each floor;
- all tradespeople, contractors and deliveries have a named employee contact who is aware of their business and supervises them while on the premises and
  - they have appointments
  - they are checked out, perhaps with references
  - there are practice guidelines for them: where they can go, what they can do, required standards of behaviour and sanctions in the contract;
- there is a procedure for dealing with unexpected callers, for example
  - they are not admitted unless they have an employee contact who will be responsible for them
  - a nominated employee (manager) sees all other unexpected callers
  - security staff/volunteers can be called to ensure people leave if necessary.

Dealing with access points other than main doors can be difficult. It is often hard to persuade staff to keep back doors and side entrances locked. It is not unusual to find one-way fire doors propped open for the convenience of staff. Apart from breaking fire regulations this leaves the building open to the world. Delivery or loading bays, vehicle entrances, service entrances and car park doors are also potential access points that people rarely think of controlling from the point of view of staff safety.

Employers can and should insist that fire doors are at least kept shut at all times; they should not be used as normal exits unless this is unavoidable.

All other side doors, rear doors, doors to car parks or garages can be self-closing/self-locking doors or they can be self-closing one-way doors like fire doors. Staff may need to be provided with keys or key cards or they may have to learn an entry code if such a system is used.

Delivery or loading bays, vehicle entrances and service entrances are sometimes more difficult to deal with directly. What has proved successful for organizations is to isolate these work areas from the rest of the workplace. So rather than controlling access to them access from them into other areas of the workplace is controlled by the use of locked doors. Access to these areas can also be controlled if it is possible to do so by using enclosing fences or otherwise enclosing them.

THE ENVIRONS OF THE WORKPLACE

Employers and employees sometimes forget that the environs of the workplace – the grounds, gardens and parking areas – are still part of the premises and need to be looked at from the point of view of safety. Even where the surrounding areas are not part of the employer's premises employee safety in these areas should still be considered; after all they are only there because their place of work is there.

Visibility is an important issue in grounds and car parks: people need to be able to see and be seen. Proper lighting is an essential part of ensuring visibility but it will only be of limited use if people are obscured by walls, fencing or vegetation. It may be necessary to consider opening up areas or barriers by removing walls and fences and keeping hedges and bushes pruned.

If car parks are multi-storey they need to be well lit everywhere, particularly in stairways. If the employer does not own the car park that employees must use then representation should be made to the owners so it can be made safer.

Some organizations provide preferential parking for women drivers so they can be nearer to the buildings and avoid parking in the potentially more risky areas. Indeed some organizations earmark all their immediate parking for women drivers while men must park in public car parks when space in the private car park is not available.

In one organization the only access to the private rooftop car park after office hours was via a public multi-storey car park that was dark, dingy and threatening for most people. As staff who travelled during the day on business by train often returned after office hours the organization agreed to pay for them to park at the station, even though it was very close to the free, private car park.

Sometimes protecting the grounds and car parks of a workplace with fencing or walls is feasible and worthwhile. An entry card system can be used with gates or barriers to allow employees' vehicles through or there can be a control operated by security staff.

Video surveillance of grounds and car parks is now more common. It enables security or other designated staff to see what is happening outside from a safe point. Any incident can be reported immediately and/or the security staff can go to the aid of someone in difficulty.

Think also about items left around in car parks or grounds; all sorts of everyday items are potential weapons. Some, such as gardening tools, are very dangerous when misused.

Sensor-activated additional lighting may also be useful as staff can run into brightly lit areas. It may also signal to security staff or others inside that something is wrong. External alarm points known to staff could be activated if help were needed. Emergency lighting is worth considering in case of power failure.

INTERVIEWING

Interviewing, or similar meetings with people, is a task that many employees in all sorts of organizations perform in the course of their work.

There have been unfortunate incidents of aggressive and violent behaviour in interviews in many different work settings. The good practice guidelines are derived from this wide range of experience in workplaces as diverse as banks, social services departments, estate agents, social security offices and police stations.

- Make sure the interview is not conducted in isolation, i.e.

  - make sure someone knows where you are;
  - use a room in which you are visible to others, for example, with glass panels (NB safety glass in the walls is essential) but where the interviewee cannot be overheard.

108

- 'Phones cause interruptions and so are often not available as a lifeline in an interview room – if this is the case there should be an alarm or panic button.

- If you cannot be easily seen in a room devise a checking procedure such as someone looking in on you, or try popping out from time to time – but try to keep interruptions to a minimum.

- Make sure the room is well lit but not glaring; emergency lights may be needed too.

- Stay near the door – if possible have two doors in the room.

- All sorts of everyday equipment can provide potential weapons so keep equipment to the absolute essentials.

- Ensure furniture is comfortable but robust enough not to be thrown.

- Make sure someone knows exactly who you are interviewing – and make sure the interviewee knows that their presence is a matter of record.

- At the first sign you are in difficulty (because people can see or hear you or you raise the alarm) staff should know who will respond and how and take immediate action.

- Do not arrange to meet anyone when you will be alone in the building.

- Prevent waiting time before an interview where possible. If there is waiting time make sure the interviewee knows when they are likely to be seen and keep them informed.

- If you expect an interview to be difficult do it at a time of day when you are at your best and if you know a client has a bad time of day avoid that.

- Don't try to blind an interviewee with science; use language they can understand but don't be condescending or talk down to them.

- Shake hands and introduce yourself by name, explain who you are in terms of your job if they don't know.

- If you escort an interviewee to a room walk with them on the level, go in front upstairs and walk behind coming downstairs.

- If the interviewee is reacting badly to you for reasons of your sex, age, class and so on hand them over to someone else with their agreement.

- If you know an interviewee has been aggressive or violent in the past, find out about the incident if possible; it may help you to plan for and manage your interview with them.

- Beware if you are told of previous aggression and violence; it could be exaggerated and adversely affect your approach to an interview.

- Think about your clothing. Obviously your dress and appearance is up to you but you may wish to consider avoiding:

  - clothing that could be provocative in a sexual or financial sense;
  - ties, blouses with ties, necklaces and so on that could be used to strangle;
  - earrings that can be pulled or torn off;
  - long hair that can be caught;
  - shoes that mean you can't run.

- Think about your position in relation to the interviewee:
  - seats of equal height;
  - seats at a 45 degree angle are less threatening; opposite is confrontation; side by side cooperation;

- you may want a desk between you and the interviewee for safety but it could also be a barrier;
- aggressive or violent people have a wider than normal buffer zone and may need more space.

- Think about taking notes to show you are taking the interviewee seriously but make sure they do not suspect a lack of interest on your part or that you are compiling a secret dossier of some sort. This can also help in keeping appropriate levels of eye contact.

- If you are both standing try to be relaxed; match your position with the interviewee.

- Do not stand over a seated interviewee: it gives the impression of crowding, superiority or greater power.

- Try to calm aggression by using sympathy, empathy, paraphrasing what was said to show you understand.

- Try to solve problems immediately, if only minor ones – to demonstrate you are helping and trying to find solutions.

- Depersonalize issues: if you are governed by rules of some sort explain that and the limits of your discretion.

- On the other hand presenting yourself as a person rather than an official can help, especially if you can convey the upset or hurt that abuse or aggression causes you personally.

- Avoid provocative expressions such as 'calm down', 'don't be silly'.

- More calming approaches include 'we' (share the problem) in 'the position we are in . . .', 'we need to . . .', or 'we can tackle it in this way . . .'

- Don't make promises you can't keep.

- Never get drawn into aggression – do not use insults, swear, threaten or ridicule.

- Don't set deadlines such as 'if you don't stop in two minutes I'll leave' – you may not be able to keep them or you will irritate the interviewee.

- Listen, and show you are listening by nodding; words such as 'yes' and 'I see' indicate attention too.

- Adopt a relaxed posture, open rather than a closed, arms-folded approach.

- Avoid tapping pens, fiddling with anything or doodling.

- If the situation is escalating try taking a break; the change may help defuse things. You could simply stretch your legs or go for a cup of tea or change venue.

OTHER PEOPLE'S HOMES

One of the causes of aggressive and violent behaviour is when people feel that there is an intrusion into their private life. Certain occupations require employees to go into the homes of other people, for example:

community nursing staff	surveyors
doctors	estate agents
social workers	insurance advisors/assessors
police officers	financial advisors
education welfare staff	trades people providing estimates
housing staff	gas and electricity staff
building inspectors	rent or other collectors of money

The potential for violence against employees in other people's homes may depend on why the employee is there. An estate agent helping to sell the property may be much more welcome than a building inspector preventing a change or extension to the property. A police officer returning stolen property may get a very different reception from a social worker taking a child into care.

Whatever the reason for being in someone else's home the cardinal rule is to remember that it is their home, their territory and you are going into it.

Under 'normal' circumstances people are in control of their homes and what happens there; your presence may change that. People may feel that you are invading their space, taking away their power, imposing rules and regulations on them or, quite literally, taking over.

Where there may be a need to go to other people's homes in order to do your job, consider the following points:

- Do you actually have to go to the other person's home? Could an arrangement be made whereby transport is provided to bring that person to you? This may be particularly worth consideration if there is a history of poor relationships with the person or aggressive and violent behaviour; or if the purpose of the visit is likely to cause problems.

- Do you have to go alone to someone's home? You could think about taking a colleague with you, although this may be difficult when resources are scarce and work loads heavy. Perhaps other possibilities could include taking a friend who would wait outside or using a taxi that would wait for you.

- Before you visit someone at home check if that person has a record of violence. If there is no record (perhaps such records should be considered) ask other colleagues who have had dealings with the person concerned.

- Before leaving your workplace make sure people know where you are going, what your plans are and when you expect to finish a visit and/or return to the workplace. Also, arrange to check in with someone at the workplace. Make sure you take with you notes of telephone numbers and money or a card for the 'phone if you do not have access to a mobile 'phone.

- Employers could consider providing mobile 'phones or two-way radios for use by staff on such occasions

- Go in daylight.

- When you arrive at the home think about its location. Is it at the top of a tower block, down a country lane, in a one-way street? Consider where you should park your car so you can leave quickly or the nearest route to public transport or a busy, well lit place.

- At the person's home remember you are the visitor; say who you are, where you are from and show some identity if you have it. Don't make assumptions; follow these guidelines:

  - check who you are talking to;
  - make sure you are expected or at least that it is understood why you are there;

111

- don't march in; wait to be asked or ask if you can go in;
- whenever possible acknowledge it is the other person's home and territory, let them lead the way, take your coat, invite you to sit down, introduce other people;
- if you get an aggressive reception at the door or the householder appears to be drunk or otherwise in a bad way you could decide not to enter the house or leave immediately without conducting your business;
- take only what is essential into a house; leave handbags, briefcases and so on elsewhere. Avoid also taking anything that you would not wish a householder to see or read;
- in the house take in your surroundings; if at all possible place yourself with a clear line to an exit;
- try to avoid reacting to the house itself, for example, if it smells, is very untidy or dirty;
- at all times remain alert to changes in moods, movements and expressions;
- do not spread your belongings about; if you need to leave quickly you will not have a chance to collect them;
- if you feel at risk – leave as quickly as possible. If you are prevented from leaving you may wish to try to control the situation (see Chapter 11, In the Event – Coping with Violence) or you may have to fight back;
- do what you have to to protect yourself – you must not worry about failure.

OTHER PEOPLE'S PREMISES

Going to conduct business on other people's premises is, to an extent, like going to other people's homes. It is their territory, not yours and you may be more or less welcome depending on the nature of your visit.

Many of the points made in the previous section apply to visiting or working in others' premises; in addition you should bear in mind the following:

- If a stranger rings to arrange a meeting it should be a routine procedure to call back to check the details of the name, company, address, telephone number and so on.

- If you have any doubts or concerns on arrival at any meeting telephone your workplace and leave details of where you are and how you can be contacted. Make it obvious that your whereabouts and schedule are known.

- You could have a previously agreed 'distress' signal so that you can summon help without compromising your safety.

- Only go to other people's premises in normal working hours when the premises are in use.

- When you are on the premises try to ensure you know where you are and how to get out.

- If you are in a quiet or isolated part of the premises, stay where you can get to an exit; preferably sit close to a door.

- Make sure you know in advance how you will get back to your workplace, i.e. means of transport.

- If you are in any doubt leave the premises if you can; if you cannot get out make as big a fuss as you need to attract attention and get help.

- If you have previously had concerns or problems or been harassed in any way when visiting or working in particular premises do not hide it because you feel a failure or silly. Tell colleagues or superiors, and arrange for someone else to go with you or instead of you next time.

- Avoid going out for meals or to other sites with anyone you are not absolutely sure about. If you must go make sure you let your workplace know your plans and that the person/s you are with are aware that you have done this.

PATTERNS OF WORK

In some types of businesses or services overtime, working late or early morning work are part of the normal working pattern; in other situations such arrangements occur on a less regular basis. Whatever patterns apply, good practice takes account of the following:

- the provision of transport for employees, especially women, when they are required to work unsocial hours and travel in darkness, when it is very quiet and when there is little public transport;

- the provision of nearby, well lit or controlled car parking;

- the use of security staff, particularly when premises are isolated, few people are actually working, at night, in areas of high risk or in business/services prone to attack, for example because they collect cash;

- alarm systems that can remain activated in parts of premises not in use while other parts are in use;

- panic buttons or alarms that can be activated in parts of premises in use even when the main alarm system is unarmed;

- ensuring people work in pairs at least and they know who else is/should be on the premises;

- making sure people are aware of any callers, contractors, deliveries and so on that are expected.

HANDLING MONEY OR VALUABLES

The handling of money or valuables is not confined to building societies and banks or the more obvious types of business such as retailing. Many companies hold cash for certain purchases or wages; and other organizations receive money, such as courts receive fines. Others actually produce valuables such as jewellers or printers of bonds and banknotes.

113

The risks associated with handling money or valuables are in three main areas: collecting, storing and moving.

Collecting Money

Collecting money in premises such as shops, building societies, pubs, garages, banks, sports centres, rent offices and so forth normally involves the use of a till or cash drawer. The sorts of precautions that can be taken to protect staff are very varied; what is required in any given situation will depend on the circumstances. Examples of precautions are as follows:

- Screens such as are seen in post offices, banks and building societies can be used to protect staff from being grabbed, having missiles thrown at them, having substances (for example ammonia) thrown at them or being directly attacked.

- Tills or cash drawers can be protected by guards so it is difficult for a thief to grab the contents; however this will probably not protect staff.

- Members of staff may be attached to the till by a key and chain; this may be effective security in one sense but it may make it difficult for staff to escape if an incident occurs. A would-be thief may also use staff as a means of getting at the till contents because they have keys.

- Tills should be emptied regularly making it far less worthwhile for a thief to steal from them.

- In the event of violent behaviour staff should know exactly what to do. Produce guidelines for staff making sure that the most important rule is to keep themselves safe, not the money or valuables.

- Alarms should be available to staff collecting money. It may be wise to have an alarm they can activate secretly to summon help. It is also sensible to make other alarm systems obvious to all.

- Security cameras are increasingly used but in order to provide immediate help to someone at risk they must be monitored constantly.

- Signs should be visible, clearly explaining security systems like cameras, time-lock safes or screens that can serve as a deterrent to some thieves.

- In some premises a highly sophisticated system of metal screens that come down on counters, doors or windows can be worthwhile. However, you could end up isolating people in an area with a potentially violent person.

- Controlling access to premises is a technique often used in banks in mainland Europe so that at any one time only a certain number of people are in the bank. As people leave, others are let in and dealt with almost immediately. They can all be observed at one time.

Other collections of money

Sometimes collecting money does not take place on the employer's premises, for example rent collections or collections for milk or newspapers delivered to individual houses. Points worth noting in these cases are as follows:

114

- If collections are made by people on their own it may be worth considering whether they should be, especially in 'high risk' areas or on dark winter afternoons. Collecting less frequently by two people could be much safer.

- Paying-in money regularly means that collectors carry far less and they are less worth stealing from; it may take longer but is a wise precaution.

- Ensure people are clear about how to proceed in the event of an approach or attack; provide guidelines that stress they should protect themselves rather than their takings.

- Provide a means for the employee to keep in contact, such as a mobile 'phone or two-way radio. Their safety can then be checked; they can raise the alarm or call for help.

- Providing personal alarms can be helpful, as long as they can be carried and people know how to use them.

- If a vehicle is used in the collecting process employees should take precautions such as locking it, parking within sight, checking it before getting in and keeping doors locked when in it.

- Consider whether it is really necessary to collect money in this way. Could a monthly bill be issued and a cheque sent instead? Could you make arrangements for people to call at a local shop, library, community centre or similar location to pay regular bills?

Storing Money

Keeping money on the premises is not just a feature of the more obvious businesses such as banks, building societies, shops and stores. Factories, offices, places of entertainment, local authorities, hospitals and many other places store money or valuables.

Where money or valuables are stored as part of the business there are usually very sophisticated forms of security. In premises where money or valuables are only held irregularly, at certain times or for certain purposes the security is often less well organized.

If you store money or valuables:

- Consider whether you actually need to do so – don't unless you must. For example have wages made up by the bank or bureau and delivered and issued immediately.

- If you collect money take it to the bank each day rather than store it.

- Use a safe and whatever security measures the circumstances demand, such as alarms, cameras, screens.

- Let the security measures be obvious.

- Make sure, through providing guidelines, that employees know what to do to protect themselves if the need arises.

- Restrict and control access to the premises, or that part of it where money or valuables are kept.

- Avoid developing a pattern of storing money, for example, when wages are to be paid.

- If storing money or valuables is your business, or if you have to store a valuable commodity, seeking specialist security advice is worthwhile. This needs to deal with the practical security measures *and* the safety of employees.

115

Moving Money

If moving money or valuables to and from your premises is a regular feature of your business it is often well worth employing a specialist security firm to do the job. It may seem costly but could be much less costly than the serious injury, or even death, of an employee.

Even if employees move the money it is worth obtaining specialist advice from a security firm or the police on your particular situation and the risks inherent in it.

Where employees do move money some general pointers to safer practice are:

- Provide guidelines for staff so that they know what to do to protect themselves; make sure they are quite clear that is their first duty, not to protect the money.

- Never send one person alone if at all possible.

- Never establish a pattern of moving money: change the days, time of day, vary the route used, walk one day and drive another, use a vehicle if possible to minimize exposure, use different branches of the bank. Also vary the people who carry money so no-one becomes a target.

- Provide people moving money with a means of contact such as a mobile 'phone or two-way radio. This ensures they can keep in touch, raise an alarm or summon help.

- Let the bank or other premises to which they are going know they are on the way and when to expect them – they can then raise the alarm if necessary.

- Have a call-back system so that you are notified on their safe arrival.

- Think about how money or valuables are best carried. If a briefcase or bag is carried it can be snatched, if it is attached to an employee it may be safe from a snatch thief but could result in the employee being injured by someone attempting to take it.

- Arming employees in any way is not a sensible idea; they may then be committing an offence.

- Provide personal attack alarms; they are useful but only if carried ready for use and used properly.

- Make sure as few people as possible know when, how and by whom money is moved.

WORKING FROM HOME OR AT HOME

All the standard precautions recommended for safe living at home apply:

- Use only initials and surname on your doorbell and in the 'phone book. You may even decide you do not want your name on the bell and remain ex-directory so you do not appear in the 'phone book; directory enquiries will not give out your number.

- A Yale-type lock can be easily opened; fit a deadlock to British Standard 3621. Make sure the door and frame are strong enough to withstand an attack at the locking points.

- Never leave keys in 'safe' places under plant pots, on ledges or under doormats.

116

- Never give keys to people working in or delivering to your home.

- Fit a spyhole to the door.

- Ensure any callers you do not know identify themselves, and do check their identity. If you are in any doubt do not let them in.

- Fit a door chain and use it.

- All windows should have locks and be secured when you are out. Secure them also when you are in unless you want them open and can keep an eye on them.

- Draw curtains and blinds after dark; do not advertise you are alone.

- If anyone comes to the door for help such as to use the 'phone do not let them in; offer to make the call yourself.

- If you have an alarm system have panic buttons fitted by the front door, back door, bed or wherever you want them. They will operate the alarm even if it is not armed.

- If you hear strange noises outside your home do not investigate them yourself, especially after dark; call the police.

- If you lose your keys, change the locks.

- If you go away cancel papers and milk, arrange to have mail collected, ask a friend or neighbour to call in, and tell the local neighbourhood watch or local police.

In addition you may consider:

- A second 'phone line specifically for work so that you can keep your private number private; you can switch off the work line or attach it to an answering machine after work hours.

- Have a PO box number for all work-related mail so that you do not have to give out your home address.

- Only ever ask people to meet you at your home if you are completely sure you are safe.

- Meet people in public places, their office or workplace but make sure someone knows where you are, with whom, for how long and when you are expected back. Make sure the person you are meeting is aware that your whereabouts and movements are known.

- Arrange for a friend or neighbour to be a contact you can 'phone during the day and report where you are or, in case of need, who can call where you are expected to check you are safe. If you change your plans let your contact know.

- Avoid after-hours meetings.

- Do not carry your diary with you; just take the information you need. If you were missing it could help to trace you, your contacts, your movements.

- Do not go to places or areas where you feel unsafe; always opt for public places, well lighted with lots of people around rather than quiet backwaters or inner city areas with high crime rates.

- If you must go to places you feel uneasy about or to meetings after hours take someone with you.

COPING WITH VIOLENCE

No matter how aware and careful you are, how skilful you are at recognizing and avoiding danger or how well you implement calming or controlling techniques you could still find yourself faced with violent behaviour.

There is a very fine line between someone being upset, angry or giving vent to their feelings and violence directed at another person. The recipient will, to some extent, determine where that line is drawn depending on the point at which they personally feel at risk, threatened or unsafe. Here we consider possible responses to violent behaviour not involving physical attack and then responses to physical violence itself.

Violence not involving physical attack

If someone becomes abusive and threatening, consider whether or not you can cope with the situation. You should not feel you have to cope with it alone; you can seek help from other people or leave altogether. First keep calm, relax, allow yourself time to think and decide the best course of action. Ask yourself if what has occurred so far in the exchange means that someone else, especially briefed by you, would be better placed to handle the situation. Colleagues may have particular skills or experience to bring that you do not have. The situation may be such that it requires specialist help such as security or the police to eject a person; if so you should get the help quickly before the situation deteriorates.

If you decide you can cope there are a number of different approaches. One that has been found to work well is the 'control trilogy'. It has three stages: calming, reaching and controlling. Each of them is dealt with here in turn.

Calming

The purpose of the calming stage is to take the heat out of the situation and enable you to start communicating with the other person positively. The principle is to simply accept what is said, not evaluate it or respond to it at this stage. Calm yourself first, breathe steadily, relax the tension in your muscles.

Think about yourself, particularly your verbal and non-verbal communication.

- Voice – keep your voice steady and calm; maintain an even tone and pitch. Speak gently, slowly, clearly and carefully.

- Face – show that you are listening and attentive; use nods to signal you are following. Try to relax your facial muscles and convey openness and empathy with the speaker.

- Eyes – make eye contact but avoid constant eye contact that may be threatening or trigger aggression because it is perceived as staring.

- Position – try to avoid eyeball-to-eyeball positions or positions where you are higher up than the other person. Avoid barriers too if it is safe to do so.

- Posture – avoid aggressive or defensive stances such as arms folded, hands on hips or waving fingers or arms. Try to look relaxed and open.

- Space – give the aggressor plenty of space. When we are upset or angry the personal space buffer zone we require can be greater than normal and the proximity of others more threatening.

Now think about the other person; do things and encourage them to do things that will contribute to calming them such as:

- Talking – keep the aggressor talking and explaining the problem, their perception of what has happened, why they feel aggrieved and so on. Use verbal and non-verbal prompts (saying 'mmm' or 'yes' or nodding) to keep them talking. Use open questions to encourage them to talk, explain or even think out loud. All this uses up energy and helps to get pent-up frustration out of their system.

- Listen – make sure you listen; the information you gather may be useful. Make sure they know you are listening to them. Listen also for the feelings, concerns and possible intentions behind their words.

- Hear them out – let this calming phase go on as long as necessary so that the aggressor feels the whole story has been told and heard. Also hear them out from the point of view of not drawing any conclusions, trying to assess or evaluate or solve the problems at this stage. Concentrate on the aggressor and what is being said; this is their space and they will be doing most of the talking.

- Watch – as you go through the calming phase watch for changes in behaviour, for example: lowering of voice to 'normal' tone, relaxing of facial muscles, steadier breathing, change in language used, postural changes or increasing tiredness (being aggressive is tiring). These changes can signal that the aggressor is becoming calmer and more approachable.

- Resist arguing – it is very tempting to respond and become engaged in an argument especially if you are the butt of the aggression or accused in some way. Resist arguing; it is far more likely to result in conflict or confrontation than contribute to defusing the situation.

- Be yourself – do not hide behind authority, status or a job title. Try to convey who *you* are; tell the aggressor your name and ask them their name. By using your name instead of a description of your status you are presenting yourself as another human being. Later it may be important to explain what authority or status you have to reassure the person that you are in a position to act on their behalf.

Reaching

When you believe that the aggressor has calmed sufficiently (as judged by the changes you observe) you can begin to reach out and try to build bridges to enable communication. You are likely to be talking more at this stage than the calming stage as you begin to develop a dialogue.

Continue to behave as before but develop the interactions with the aggressor; you will be able to do this much more effectively if you have listened well in the calming stage, for example:

- Explain back to them what you believe they have said, what the problem is or what they require.

- Seek their confirmation of the facts or key points they have made.

- Clarify what action, assistance and so on they require.

- Encourage them into further relaxation by sitting down if this is possible and offering them refreshments.

- Try smiling in encouragement and acknowledgement as it can relax both of you but do prevent them from thinking you find the situation funny.

- Empathize with their feelings but avoid any behaviour that could be interpreted as patronizing.

- Ask any questions you need to ask but make sure they know why you need to know.

- Encourage them to relate to you: check that they remember your name, your job and how you can help them as they may have forgotten in the heat of the moment.

- Try to move physically alongside the other person if you can and you feel it is safe; this can signal an intention to work towards a solution together.

- Try to find out about the other person, particularly previous contacts or experience of your organization or other information that may help you deal with the problem.

- Encourage them to ask questions, clarify things or seek information. In replying keep it simple and straightforward and avoid jargon.

- Consider taking notes if this gives a positive impression of taking the other person seriously or being the first steps towards helping them. Do not take notes if it appears to be officialdom in action to the other person.

Controlling

Once you feel that you have established a reasonably 'normal' order of communication with the aggressor you can move into the controlling stage. This does not mean you take over and run the show! It means that you can move forward together in a controlled fashion towards a resolution of the problem. This stage requires you to maintain the calming and reaching behaviour while moving forward to actually tackling the problem. The aim of this process is win–win, both you and the other person achieving a solution that is satisfactory.

As you work with the other person towards the solution use the following approaches:

- Set targets for yourselves – set out what you need to achieve and when (i.e. immediately, later, today, by an agreed time) and make sure both of you agree to and understand what you are aiming for.

- One at a time – if the situation or problem is complex tackle each aspect separately. Agree the list of issues you need to work through with the other person.

120

- Simple first – tackle the simpler problems, issues or aspects of the situation first and quickly. Solving parts of the problem or resolving the simpler issues quickly creates a positive atmosphere by demonstrating progress.

- Complex later – move on to tackle the more complex aspects of the situation once you have made some progress and are working more effectively together. Try to divide the more complex aspects so that you can tackle them one by one or agree the steps you need to take and then go through them.

- Establish reality – be clear and honest about what you can and cannot do. Explain what is achievable, when and what is not and give the reasons; make sure the other person has realistic expectations.

- The other view – acknowledge that the other person has their own views and opinions and will want to put, and have heard, their side of the argument or their analysis of the situation. You need to understand them and help them to hear things from your side and understand you.

- Admit failings – if you or your organization has failed in some respect or caused a problem do not try to cover up. Admit where you have gone wrong and start working on putting it right. If the other person has made a mistake, misunderstood or caused the problem explain to them without blaming or causing them to feel or appear foolish.

- Avoid jargon – steer clear of organizational or bureaucratic jargon that may confuse or provoke the other person. Above all avoid defending yourself or the organization by using jargon as a shield; you will simply alienate the other person.

- Offer alternatives – if the other person's needs cannot be met (or met fully) it may help to offer alternatives. Any alternatives must be realistic and go some way towards meeting the needs. This approach may offer the other person a way out (a win) especially if they have come to realize they were at fault, that their original expectations are unrealistic or their needs cannot be met as they would wish.

- Refer to others – if you cannot solve the problem or meet the needs there may be others who can. Do not use this approach as an escape route for yourself by passing the problem on. Refer people on only where you believe they can really obtain help, advice or satisfaction. Try to ensure the person to whom you refer is available, agree a meeting if this is appropriate and pass on information that will be needed. If you can only provide details of whom they can approach then provide proper details (name, address, telephone number and so on) rather than vague directions.

- Do not hurry – even if you are busy you really have to make time to see these sorts of situations through. If you do not you may have wasted a great deal of groundwork or, worse still, left yourself or others open to future aggressive behaviour. Do not show you are pushed for time or try to force the situation along more quickly than the other person can go; that may elicit further aggression.

- Encourage – if you are making progress together express your pleasure at it, acknowledge the other person's part in that and encourage further cooperation. Encourage them also to express their feelings so that you can know if they do actually feel satisfied with a solution or progress so far, or if they are just going along with it.

- Contract – sometimes it will not be possible to solve a problem or deal with all the issues there and then as you may need time to collect information, research something and so on. Do not leave the other person feeling 'fobbed off'; think about

121

agreeing future action as a sort of contract between you. Set dates to meet, arrange to telephone or say when you will write. Agree what each of you will do. Show that you have a continuing commitment to helping them. If you do make a commitment – keep it.

- Review – at the end of the process go back and review what you have achieved, what each of you has agreed to do, any further contact you have agreed or further targets you have set.

The control trilogy is one way of coping with aggressive people. It is not particularly easy but, given time and practice, can help you think through the process of dealing with an aggressor and develop the appropriate skills to manage the situation and keep safe.

You will not always be able to go through the three stages sequentially and tidily. Very often you will find that you move back and forth between stages. As you learn to observe and predict the other person's behaviour you can react by using the techniques or approaches from each stage. For example, you may be working quite well together on a particular problem when, inadvertently, a raw nerve is touched and the other person becomes aggressive again. You may well have to go right back to basics and start calming the situation again before reaching to re-establish communication and ultimately cooperation.

If, when faced with aggression, you decide you can cope and start working through this process, remember you can stop at any time if you feel at risk or you can get help if you need it. Using the control trilogy to deal with an aggressor can be very effective but it is time-consuming and requires patience. It also requires you to put aside your feelings to some extent and make your goal that of managing the situation and resolving the problem. You may do a marvellous job and still end up feeling shaky, upset or angry yourself. Think about what you need, go and talk your experience through with someone, make sure you report the incident or ask for more specialist help if you need to.

Finally, do not assume this method will always be appropriate or succeed. Some aggressors are beyond control, particularly if they are ill, drunk or under the influence of drugs and in some work situations it is essential to remove someone creating a disruption immediately, for example in a hospital, in which case calming the aggressor is not an option.

Physical attack

Violence can take the form of physical attack, though thankfully that is a rare occurrence and the chances of the average person being attacked is once in a hundred years. However, the relative rarity of such events does not mean you should not think about and prepare for the possibility. This is particularly true if you fall outside that average category by being in a type of work where the risks are higher. Should someone launch a physical attack on you the options are limited to:

1. Getting away – escaping from the situation at the first suggestion of physical violence.

2. Fighting back and ultimately fighting free to escape.

3. Attempting to defuse or manage the situation or come to some sort of compromise by handing over what is wanted and removing the threat of violence.

Getting away

Running away is very often the best form of defence. Escape from attack can be more difficult than it sounds, though. The effect of a surprise attack can be shock that immobilizes you for a time and once you have recovered the chance to flee is lost. That is why thinking through how to react is worthwhile – it is hoped you will never need it but it is worth doing just as lifesaving and first aid are worth learning although you hope you never need them either.

There are some fairly simple things you can do to make it easier to get away should you need to:

- Practise keeping calm through breathing and relaxation exercises so you can think clearly and move when you want to.

- Wear shoes you can walk fast in. They need to be the sort of shoes that stay on your feet and are not liable to collapse if you have to run.

- Wear sensible clothing that allows you to move quickly and run and that is not readily grabbed to hold on to you or used to restrain you.

- Be realistic – it is extremely difficult to kick someone in the groin and in the attempt you may just unbalance yourself. Similarly kicking shins puts you off balance. Do not imagine you could use your fingers or some object to inflict injury, let alone use them to disable others. Scratching faces, poking eyes out and so on is not natural for most people. If you attempt it you are also vulnerable to having your hands and arms, or even your weapon, grabbed and used against you.

- Remember that lashing out with a bag, briefcase or umbrella may not be very sensible either since you could end up off balance or have your would-be weapon taken from you and used.

- Keep your eyes open in whatever environment you find yourself. Train yourself to automatically register exits, escape routes, places where there will be other people, alarm points and so on.

- Use an alarm, but remember that to use it you need to be able to get hold of it quickly. They are very loud and piercing; even though you may not find hordes rushing to your aid an alarm let off in an attacker's ear will be stunning. While the attacker is stunned you can run.

- Scream and shout as soon as you are able. In order to make a noise you need a voice and that can be the first thing to go when you are in a state of fear and shock. You need to practise breathing in deeply, letting oxygen into your system and allowing your blood to circulate properly so you can think and act. Breathing in deeply, like a deep sigh and expelling the air loudly in a bellow has a remarkable effect. When you shout you should shout something clear and significant such as an order to 'call the police' rather than 'help' which may be interpreted as larking about.

- Don't imagine you can run away with all your possessions. If, for example, you have a suitcase of heavy items, leave it behind.

- Break-away moves can be useful in giving yourself the element of surprise over the attacker and sufficient time to escape. However, you must learn to use them properly and practise them in order to be able to execute them when you want to, safely and effectively.

- Distract your attacker long enough to be able to break free. You need to be sufficiently calm and self-possessed to do this effectively.

- Make it easy for you to hand over belongings or let an attacker take them if necessary. This means carry only what you must have with you. Keep money, credit cards, cheque cards, valuables and so on in different places if you must carry them at all.

123

Fighting back – fighting free

Standing your ground and taking your chances in a fight really is a last resort when you cannot avoid it or all else has failed.

Fighting back is only a realistic response when you are trapped and it is the only remaining option. If you have to fight back the aim should be to achieve any opening so you can escape. Should you ever be in a situation where you feel you must fight off an attacker you need to remember that:

- You can defend yourself but may do only what is reasonable in the circumstances. The law permits you to defend yourself but not to take revenge upon your attacker or to use unreasonable force; such action could be construed as assault. Equally hitting out at an attacker leaving the scene could be assault.

- You may use force to defend your property provided again that force is reasonable given the circumstances.

- You may use reasonable force to detain an attacker until help or the police arrive.

- You cannot carry an offensive weapon in a public place even if you only ever intend to use it in your own defence (Prevention of Crime Act 1953). There is no such thing as a defensive weapon. You cannot, therefore, carry anything made for or adapted to cause injury. That includes articles that originally had innocent purposes but have been adapted. Note also that any article is an offensive weapon if the bearer intends to use it to cause injury. Special legislation applies to articles with blades or sharp points (Criminal Justice Act 1988 Section 139). It is an offence to carry in a public place an article which has a blade or sharp point except a folding pocket knife with a blade cutting edge of three inches or less. But if such an article, including a folding pocket knife, were made, adapted or intended to cause injury it would become an offensive weapon.

- The law does not preclude the use of innocent items for self-protection provided that the force used is reasonable. Examples include umbrellas, handbags and walking sticks. Remember though that your 'weapon' could be taken from you and used against you.

- Even if you have learned self-defence it will only be of limited use if your attacker is bigger and stronger or if there is more than one person. Learning self-defence may help you to keep your cool, keep your balance and break free to run but do not assume if will allow you to toss attackers over your shoulder!

- If it comes to a fight try to stay clear of even more dangerous spots than the one you are in; avoid being cornered, steer clear of stairways, roadsides, platform edges at stations, dark areas or objects your attacker could use. It is difficult to remember all this in the heat of the moment so simply remember to stay in as clear and open an area as possible.

- If you really do have to fight then *go for it!* Put every bit of anger and energy into your efforts and fight for your life. Forget about hurting the attacker, just do it and get away. Try to make the first blow count; you may not get another chance. Here are some tips on vulnerable parts:
  - The solar plexus is a vital striking area. It is the centre of a web of nerves and a forceful blow with an umbrella or walking stick has a paralysing effect. The attacker will feel a sense of nausea so intense that even a drunkard or a person high on drugs can be stopped.
  - The elbow joint is also very weak. Strike it with the palm of your hand when the

124

attacker's arm is straight. At the same time, jerk his wrist against the pressure. It is very painful and disabling.

- Under the armpit, slightly to the front, is an area rich in nerves and arteries and a walking stick, umbrella point, key or ballpoint pen jabbed here causes intense pain.
- Any blow to the large area running down the side of the rib cage can be painful. A palm or side of the hand, a bunch of keys, a pencil or pen, stick or umbrella, even a hardback book, especially if the strike is hard, will cause great pain.
- Try twisting the ears off or shout down them; slap both sides of the head. A sharp quick strike *between* the eyes can knock your attacker unconscious. If your life is in danger, strike hard.
- The fingers: bend any finger right back (not just a little way). Stamp on them, bite them, pull them apart. A broken finger is completely disabling.

- If you disable your attacker, run away as fast as you can. Do not stop to see what you have done or to do more. Go straight to where you will find other people and call the police immediately.

- In fighting back you risk the possibility of a charge of assault. As soon as you can make notes about what happened, when, where, witnesses and so on.

- No one can make the decision for you if you are attacked. It will be for you to judge at the time, so, unlikely as it may be that it will occur, you should try to think through what you should do. You will need to keep calm, think clearly, act quickly and decisively and get away.

Defusing the situation

Defusing the situation may not be a realistic option if the attacker is hell-bent on doing violence to you, is ill, or is under the influence of alcohol or drugs. However, many attackers are only driven to physical violence as a means to obtain what they want. You could try an initial approach to defuse the immediate circumstances and then get away.

- Calm the attacker. Try to buy some time by staying calm, asking questions, talking and so on until help arrives or you can see a means of escape.

- Refuse to be intimidated. Shouting back, becoming angry or showing confidence may deter some attackers altogether or at least give you time to run or for help to arrive.

- Give in. Hand over whatever it is the attacker wants; it is often sensible to throw whatever it is clear of you so the attacker goes for it while you escape. Do not worry about handing over your employer's property; it will be insured and its loss will be far less costly than injury to you.

If you do make any attempts of this kind you must be constantly on your guard as the situation develops. Always use whatever time or space you can create to your advantage by getting further away, near an exit, closer to other people, into the open, to an alarm and so on. Get away just as soon as you can and get help.

Self-defence

Self-defence training was something that many organizations placed great store by in recent years but, more recently still it has been the focus of much debate. Self-defence has its dangers:

- it can lead to a false sense of security and over-confidence, especially if people do not keep in practice;

- it can lead to potential victims failing to recognize opportunities to calm situations because they are busy planning their defence;

- it is a second best to an outcome where neither party suffers injury.

It also has potential benefits:

- self-protection training has helped many people by increasing their confidence and helping them develop 'automatic' responses, but it still requires regular refresher training as advised by the police;

- by using specific restraint techniques people can be prevented from doing themselves or others harm, given time to calm down, or to get help.

12
Non-verbal Communication

Incidents of violence in the workplace are very often considered to be occasions when communication of any 'normal' sort has broken down. However, it is important to remember that the violent person is, or started out by, trying to communicate. The reasons that communication has broken down may not be solely that an individual is prone to violence; it may be a result of all sorts of messages they, and others in the situation, are picking up.

As much as 90 per cent of communication is through non-verbal behaviour and so learning to read the non-verbal signs and signals can be invaluable when trying to assess situations for risk, in predicting violent outbursts and in presenting yourself.

The components of communication are often described as follows:

- verbal – representing 7 per cent of communication

- non-verbal – vocal tone, which makes up about 38 per cent of communication

- non-verbal – body language, which makes up 55 per cent of communication.

Very many different elements of verbal and non-verbal behaviour are at play in communication. People give and receive signals, whether consciously or not, and these signals can trigger a spectrum of responses from positive to negative.

RECOGNIZING SIGNALS

Knowledge of the elements of non-verbal communication can help you to develop effective communication skills by enabling you to:

- recognize danger signals from others;

- avoid stereotypical or snap judgements of other people that could trigger violence;

- be conscious that other people will receive signals from you and form impressions;

- choose to send certain signals and messages through your non-verbal behaviour.

127

Impressions and stereotypes

On meeting someone, or even speaking to them on the telephone, we have an immediate impression of them. Generally speaking we do not notice individual physical aspects of the person straight away (for example, eyes, hair); we are more likely to register their age, gender and race.

It is all too easy to make snap judgements of people on the basis of first impressions and our own stereotypes. The common reactions many people experience indicate:

woman = secretary
man = boss
young lad with long hair and earring = yob

Because of a person's colour, age or disability (we rarely see the ability) it is easy to make judgements about capability, to respond stereotypically to questions or requests or to prejudge that person's behaviour.

Others will also respond to us in this way, gaining a first impression or pigeon-holing us as a result of their stereotypes.

It is important to acknowledge that we all have first impressions and work from the basis of stereotypes. It is equally important to remember that they may be totally inaccurate or irrelevant. Our 'norm' is not necessarily the other person's 'norm' and it is therefore easy to misinterpret the signs and signals. Avoiding the possibly unproductive or even unsafe consequences of this means putting first impressions and stereotypes to one side, difficult though it is, and allowing people time to make themselves known to us before we make any decisions about them.

Dress

Many of our snap judgements about people are as a consequence of dress. We tend to make assessments on the basis of:

smart or scruffy
formal or casual
appropriate or inappropriate
old-fashioned or trendy

We also tend to react on the basis of what we like or our experiences; for example a uniform can be reassuring or threatening.

Our assessment of the person is entirely subjective and may or may not be accurate or anything like the perception the other person has of him/herself. What is smart to one person is old-fashioned to another and what is practical and appropriate to one may be scruffy or too casual to another.

How we dress is clearly our own choice unless our job demands specific clothing and we accept that condition of employment. However, like it or not, we must remember that our dress will have an impact on other people and their perceptions of us. We all have to make decisions about whether or not to choose clothing with that in mind and decide if we want to try to create a particular impression.

Wearing certain types of clothing can convey a relaxed, open, welcoming appearance, mark the person as 'one of the crowd' or send out signals that the person is businesslike, but there is no guarantee that we will always create the impression we wish.

For example, going into an organization with a serious complaint, a customer may be faced with a very smartly dressed, be-suited woman trained to smile and deal with complaints efficiently. The visitor may see an overdressed escapee from Dallas, grinning as if all were well when plainly, to the complainant, it is not.

Not everyone will be able or willing to take time or make the effort to go beyond first impressions, particularly if they are upset, annoyed or angry to start with. They may also be predisposed to misread signals from others. The appropriateness of clothing is thus important: people can be helped to relate more readily to others if they are not surprised or confused by the signals sent out. It is up to individuals to decide to what extent they will accommodate the expectations of other people and the context in which they are relating to them.

The issue of dressing safely is a contentious one, particularly for women. Certainly women should be free to choose what they wear but it is essential to bear in mind that messages intended may not be the ones that are received by other people. Although it curtails individual freedom, a decision to dress differently may be essential to minimize risk.

It is not just clothes themselves that convey messages to others. Carrying a briefcase or clip-board can be seen as efficient or officious; wearing badges or insignia (including the old school tie!) can bring recognition and acceptance or aversion.

Eye contact

Appropriate eye contact is a very important element of communication. If you look at someone constantly you will soon find that they become uncomfortable. People do not generally like to be stared at, peered at or be the subject of a penetrating gaze. Too much eye contact can be interpreted as being threatening or overbearing and can trigger aggressive responses.

Too little eye contact may lead people to believe that you are not listening to them, not paying attention or not taking them seriously and can also lead to an aggressive reaction.

Appropriate eye contact for the vast majority of people means keeping it regular, but not constant. A speaker will look away from a listener, but will establish direct eye contact from time to time to see that the listener is attentive, is understanding what is being said, to pick up clues about the listener's reactions and to modify what is being said if necessary.

A listener makes eye contact to demonstrate attentiveness and understanding but can also convey discomfort or confusion, boredom or other reactions to the speaker.

People's eyes can be extremely expressive and show humour, fear, distress, shyness, excitement and so on. Eye contact enables us to pick up these signals, and in combination with other signals, realize how we are affecting the other person or assess how well we are communicating. This allows us to modify our behaviour and to recognize changes in the other person on which we may choose to or need to act.

You can learn to convey certain messages by practising in front of a mirror and using your eyes to express what you want. This can be useful in difficult situations because you can avoid being 'given away' by your eyes when you have learnt to adopt a calm, steady look and can maintain regular eye contact even under stress.

Facial expressions

Our facial expressions can convey a great deal about the way we are thinking and feeling. Eyes and mouths are probably the most expressive features that can show feelings on our faces that we are denying with our words.

129

Facial expressions show everything from terror to total calm and they can change very quickly too as our thoughts and feelings change.

Reading people's facial expressions can help in recognizing when they are upset, angry or annoyed even if their words are not expressing these feelings. It is often possible to see tension or anger building up on someone's face long before they express it verbally so you can be forewarned of possible danger and take appropriate action.

Your facial expression may also betray feelings that you would prefer to keep to yourself or you may wish to learn to recognize and adopt particular facial expressions in certain circumstances. You can learn about your own expressions by sitting in front of a mirror and practising looking tense, relaxed, upset, calm, angry and so on, so that you come to recognize the feeling of each and can learn to adopt expressions that will help you when communicating with others.

Body posture/movement

Posture and body movements can convey an enormous range of messages about how a person is feeling, their mood, their attitudes and how they are relating to others. Sometimes the messages are intended, like a wave, while sometimes they are not, like nervous fiddling in an interview.

Gestures and movements also have acquired meanings that are understood generally, such as 'thumbs up' or by particular groups such as secret signs of a gang of children. Some gestures and movements have meaning in one society or culture and no meaning, or a different meaning, in others.

In some cases posture, gestures or movements may have simply become habits and are not intended to convey anything, though other people may still read meaning into them.

While observing and endeavouring to understand the messages given by posture and body movements is important in communication it is also necessary to remember how easy it can be to misread or misinterpret the messages. Sometimes it is as well to check your understanding by asking the other person how they feel or what they are thinking. Some of the ways in which people may convey messages through posture and body movements are as follows:

- Anxious
  - clenched hands;
  - pulling at clothing;
  - fiddling – with hair, pen and so on;
  - fidgeting – changing position;
  - frowning;
  - biting lips.

- Depressed
  - slumped in a chair;
  - downcast;
  - shoulders hunched;
  - not responding;
  - over-the-top bright and breezy manner.

- Disapproving
  - pulling away;
  - folded arms;
  - stiff, upright, looking down;
  - raised eyebrows.

130

- Frustrated
  - sighing;
  - eyes raised skywards;
  - shaking of head;
  - jerky movements of hands such as tapping.

- Aggressive
  - clenched fists or flexing hands;
  - finger wagging or jabbing;
  - shaking of head;
  - arm waving;
  - rigid posture, tense muscles.

- Threatened
  - closed posture, arms folded, legs crossed;
  - averted gaze, head turned away;
  - backing away.

- Relaxed
  - open posture, arms at side;
  - smiling, head up and making eye contact;
  - flowing movements, not jerky or sudden.

Learning to read the messages given by posture and body movements can help you to recognize how other people are feeling and reacting in the course of communication. You can then make decisions about your own behaviour that may increase the effectiveness of communication by relaxing, calming or reassuring the other person. If the messages you receive are danger signals then you can respond in the most appropriate way to keep yourself safe by defusing the aggression, getting help or getting away.

You can also learn about your own posture and body movements by observing yourself; video is effective for this. You may decide to avoid certain habits of behaviour that convey messages you do not wish to convey. For example, many of us point or wave fingers in excitement or to add weight to what we are saying. Our listeners may well receive the gesture as aggressive or overbearing.

You could also learn behaviour that will be helpful in certain circumstances. For example, you can learn how to hold yourself and what to do with your hands to avoid appearing nervous and fidgeting in difficult situations such as interviews or when someone is complaining to you.

Reading the messages in posture and body movement is a skill that can be learnt and applied but care must be taken to avoid reading too much into what you observe or assuming you are always correct in your reading. Cultural differences, regional differences, individual habits and your own approach, preferences and attitudes all complicate the process, so check your understanding with the other person.

Space

Communication between people can be very significantly affected by the way in which the space around them, and what they consider to be their space, is treated by others.

Personal space

Each of us has around us a zone of personal space; for some people the zone is very large and for others it is only small. It can feel very offensive or aggressive if someone comes too close and invades this invisible buffer zone. Of course loved ones and close friends are welcomed into the personal space but others may not be. The invasion of personal space by strangers can feel very threatening, create tension or lead to upset or anger. If someone invades your personal space you arc likely to want to back away and re-establish the space between you; if the person follows you may end up feeling pursued or cornered. On the other hand too much distance between two people trying to communicate can seem like a gulf and make each feel as if the other is unapproachable or inaccessible.

Getting the balance right means being very sensitive to the other person's signals so that you can be close enough to avoid feelings of distance without intruding on their personal space. You will often find that you can be physically closer to someone standing up than you can sitting down; people generally seem to require a larger buffer zone when seated.

Spatial relationship

Just as the distance between yourself and another person is important, so is the relationship, or orientation, in space. Sitting side by side with another person is usually recognized as a cooperative relationship where you are working together as equals. Sitting opposite someone can seem authoritarian, official, formal, competitive or, especially when a desk is used, as putting up barriers. When in a group sitting in a circle can signal that everyone has an equal, if different, contribution to make. Sitting in rows in a formal setting tends to put the power in the hands of a leader and leave it there, and makes getting to know people and forming relationships more difficult. The height at which people sit is significant too, try to ensure you sit at the same height as the person you are talking to. A higher position tends to signal superiority and inferiority in the relationship even if this is not intended.

Territory

Another form of space around us is territory. It is a wider area or place that we regard as ours and as where we belong: perhaps a room at home, our office or the area around our desk at work. Our expectation is that, as ours, this territory will be respected and not invaded by others. We are all likely to react adversely if we find someone going through our things, using our things or otherwise invading the territory.

When jobs entail working in other people's homes or premises, particularly where this involves inspection, enforcement or other duties that may be unwelcome, it is not unusual to find that people can become violent. Part of the reaction may well be because their territory is invaded and they have little or no power to prevent it. If you are entering other people's territory it is important to realize that there may be adverse reactions; so take sensible precautions, such as not going alone.

Touch

As part of communication, touch has an important role in showing love, support, concern, empathy, encouragement and so on, as well as the simpler purposes such as greeting with a handshake or a congratulatory pat on the back.

The acceptability of different kinds of touch varies between individuals, cultures and other groups and we learn what is appropriate and what is not through observation, experience and reading the signals we receive from others.

Some people will not like to be touched at all; they may be distressed by it or feel threatened and could react aggressively. Some people feel unable to touch because they are unsure of how it will be received or it may seem 'unprofessional' in some settings or 'sloppy'. Others, however are uninhibited and spontaneous about touching. There are also people who may well want the comfort or reassurance of touch but may be unable to signal that is what they need.

Touch is an area requiring careful consideration of the other person's needs. It can be patronizing, offensive, feel like an invasion of personal space or even recall unpleasant and traumatic memories. On the other hand touch can be the most effective way of showing genuine care and concern for another person and establishing a bond with them.

One way to discover if touch is needed and welcome is to observe the other person carefully while offering limited support such as a hand on their arm. They will signal their comfort or discomfort and you can decide whether to move away or put a comforting arm around their shoulders.

Voice

In communication what is most important may not be what you say but the way that you say it, or hear it. Tone of voice, pitch, speed, rhythm and accent can all play a part in the communication process over and above the words. To communicate effectively you should avoid the following:

- making assumptions about people because of their accent;

- making assumptions based on nationality or race; people are not dangerous because they sound excited or stupid because they speak English as a second language;

- lapsing into a clinical or detached response to people where your voice has little tone or rhythm and you convey disinterest or boredom;

- letting your tension get the better of you and betraying your feelings because your voice becomes higher pitched, you adopt an excited tone or start to gabble;

- a supercilious tone, as there is little more likely to trigger a violent reaction than the other person feeling put down, foolish or wrong;

- mumbling or speaking too quickly because being unable to hear properly or follow what is said is irritating and frustrating to the listener;

- showing your views and feelings in your tone (for example contempt or sarcasm) but not in your words; the listener is still more than likely to pick up your signals and respond in kind.

In dealing with others watch for the following:

- raised voice, rapid speech and gabbling, as this signals rising tension;

- changes in tone and pitch as the conversation progresses that may suggest anger, frustration or impending violent behaviour;

- slow, menacing tones that, despite the words, demonstrate that the speaker is angry and likely to erupt into violent behaviour.

One of the most useful of skills is to be able to control your voice in difficult or threatening situations. Your aim is to be calm, clear, firm and polite even if the other person is none of these things. You can practise this using a tape recorder to get accustomed to your own voice and to try out and learn calm, clear, firm and polite responses. Another way is to work with other people and roleplay situations so that you can practise responding appropriately.

133

Listening

Listening is an essential part of communicating effectively. It can be passive, but to be really effective it needs to be, and be seen to be, active. On the one hand active listening implies letting the speaker know you are listening and following what is said by sounds you make (mmm, yes) and the gestures or feedback (nodding your head, smiling acknowledgement) you use. This confirms for the speaker that you are attentive.

On the other hand active listening is about the process of picking up non-verbal signals, assessing the messages in and behind words and putting all the non-verbal information together with the verbal to build up a complete picture of what is being said.

Listening actively to someone can be very important, first of all to them, because:

- it shows they are being given the space to say what they want to say;

- they are being given time and attention by someone;

- it demonstrates that what they say is felt to be worth listening to;

- it avoids feelings of being fobbed off, frustration and anger.

It is important also to you, because:

- it allows you to focus attention on that person and nothing else;

- you can concentrate on both the verbal and non-verbal communication together and form a more accurate view of the problem or issue and the person's feelings;

- it avoids misunderstanding or partial understanding and so can save time and problems;

- it makes it possible to respond sensibly and sensitively to the other person;

- it gives you a better chance of predicting behaviour that may put you at risk.

Making time to listen actively to someone can help establish a relationship and cooperation. Someone who has been listened to and feels they have been heard is more likely to accept a less than ideal solution to a problem than someone who feels they have not had a chance to explain or been given explanations in return.

13
Helping Yourself – Recognizing and Avoiding Danger

Even if you work in an organization that has well developed policies and procedures designed to combat violence they cannot guarantee the safety of every individual in every situation. Nor do they remove the responsibility of every individual to take care of themselves and to ensure their own safety as far as possible.

Most people tend to operate from a basis of expectations and assumptions that most other people will behave within certain norms. When situations are, or become, violent the initial feelings generally include surprise and shock because the violent behaviour is unexpected. In many cases, looking back, victims of violence can identify signs or signals that led up to the outburst; some victims even comment 'I should have realized'. Hindsight is all very well but knowing how to recognize the danger beforehand and act on the recognition is what is really useful in keeping safe.

It is difficult to strike a balance between being cautious and being suspicious and between consciously assessing the risks and always expecting trouble. It is, however, possible to develop skills, behaviour and ways of working that will help you in recognizing and avoiding danger based on awareness and confidence rather than paranoia! Here are some suggestions.

SELF AWARENESS

Feelings

Feelings and emotions rarely seem to be welcome in the workplace and it is rarer still to find that people are encouraged to acknowledge them or talk about them, let alone act on them. Being conscious of the way you feel can however help keep you safe, either directly because you acknowledge fear or concern and act on it or indirectly because you can acknowledge feelings of anger or tension in yourself that may trigger or escalate the behaviour of others.

Consider whether or not you recognize and pay attention to your feelings and instincts. If you feel anxious or fearful it may be that you dismiss the feelings as 'foolish' rather than acknowledging them and taking time to establish why you feel this way and what action you should take. You can subconsciously register threat or risk because you are picking up signals from around you or from other people without allowing yourself to become conscious of them and deal with them.

For example: is the creepy feeling in the car park or underpass really silly? Should you acknowledge that the feeling is triggered by the anxiety or fear of what may lurk in the darkness or round the corners or because there is no attendant or means of calling to other people? The potential danger may mean you choose a safer route or parking place where you do not feel at risk.

Again, if you feel nervous, you have butterflies and your heart is thumping it may seem you are over-reacting to a red-faced, finger-wagging person shouting at you. Stop and think, though; their signals may suggest impending violent behaviour and your instincts to leave or get help may be quite right.

Sometimes disregarding feelings, because acting on them seems silly or you think other people will think you foolish, is the least safe way to behave. Use your feelings to help you decide what makes you feel safe and confident and then do it.

Knowing how you are feeling can also help you to plan ways of working to keep yourself safe. If you are tired, anxious, angry or overstressed it is sensible to acknowledge the way you feel and avoid situations that you may be unable to deal with effectively. For example:

- A complaining customer or client who has been abusive to you in the past and with whom you still feel angry appears: get someone else to see them.

- If you have to reach agreement with other people on a difficult issue choose a time when you feel calm, confident and relaxed.

- If something must be done, or somebody dealt with *now* and you do not feel able, think about getting help or asking someone else to do it rather than put yourself or others at risk.

Ways of Working

Many of us do our jobs the way that we have always done them without ever taking time to think about whether we are putting ourselves at risk unnecessarily. Some of the things to consider when assessing the possible risks in the way you work are:

- Does anyone know where you are?

- If you change your plans, do you inform people?

- Do you check or vet people that you go to meet alone?

- Can you be contacted?

- Is there a check-in system and do you use it?

- Do you think about where you park – is it safe?

- Do you use the quickest routes or the safest?

- Do you carry money or valuables?

- Are you alone at work at all?

- Are you protected from members of the public properly?

- Do you carry an alarm?

136

- Would anyone miss you? How long would it be before you were missed? Could you be found?

Think about the fact that the most straightforward, resource-efficient way of working may not be the safest way. For example, going with a colleague to certain places or to meet certain people may be much safer than going alone even though it means taking the time of two people. Taking short cuts when you are busy and in a hurry may mean you cannot be contacted, you are isolated or in unsafe areas; it is better to be late than not arrive at all.

The more you work independently or autonomously the more you need to think about how you work and build in safety precautions. No matter how hard others strive to ensure your safety the key role in your safety is yours.

Physical well-being

Your physical well-being can have a significant impact on your safety, and not just how fast you can run away!

If you are unfit, overtired or stressed you are less likely to have the energy and attention to put into ensuring your own safety. You may become less able to deal with difficult people or situations or more prone to escalate difficult situations into dangerous ones.

Think about aspects of your physical well-being: learn to recognize when you are feeling down, achy, sluggish or over-tired and start looking after yourself. For example:

- Eating properly – have a sensible, varied, balanced diet. Eat regularly and take time to eat meals. Avoid too much fat, sugar and stimulants such as alcohol.

- Exercise – take regular, daily exercise such as a brisk walk, a daily swim or get an exercise machine. Half an hour a day can make a big difference.

- Sleep well – make sure you allow yourself the sleep you need. Relax before going to bed, have a bath, read or have a soothing drink but avoid alcohol or sleeping pills.

- Relax – take up a hobby that is relaxing and learn yoga or meditation. Make time to go out and do things and be with people. Set a time each day to listen to music, lie on a sunbed or pamper yourself by doing something you want to do.

Messages you give

How do you think other people perceive you and understand you from the messages you give? Do you give the appearance of being confident, assured, pleasant and competent? Are you likely to be perceived as nervous, uneasy, uncomfortable or unsure?

Much research into victim psychology and the types of people who are mugged or attacked suggests that the messages we give can have an effect on the likelihood, or otherwise, of being the subject of other people's violence. People who convey by their posture, movement, demeanour and behaviour that they are confident are less likely to be victims. Some ways of conveying self-assurance and confidence include:

- Stand tall and straight rather than hunched.

- Walk steadily, maintaining a rhythm rather than stumbling along.

- Keep your head up; look ahead not down.

- Pay attention to your surroundings: if you look alert and aware you are less vulnerable but avoid looking shyly or nervously around.

- Know where you are going; avoid looking lost or disoriented.

- Avoid eye contact with other people.

- Look calm and serious as if knowing what you are about and in control.

- Avoid giving the impression of being tense or nervous by wringing your hands, fidgeting or fiddling.

- Keep yourself balanced by having your weight evenly on both feet; you will look and feel steady and secure.

AWARENESS OF OTHERS

Relating to others

Like everyone else you will have first impressions of people or make certain assumptions about them. These impressions and assumptions are very immediate; they may be right or wrong and may change or not as you interact with the other person. The impressions and assumptions can sometimes help you to make judgements about your own safety and help you avoid danger. In some ways it does not matter if you are right or wrong or doing an injustice to the other person because, for your own safety, it is as well not to wait to find out how accurate or fair you are. For example, a woman walking on her own at night may see a group of apparently drunken youths approaching and feel threatened. They may be very nice young lads having a good time but they may not. The wisest action is probably to assume the worst and change direction.

Your impressions and assumptions can be based on prejudices and generalizations that bear little resemblance to reality. The consequences can be that your behaviour towards people (body language, voice, eye contact, manner) based on assumptions, prejudices or stereotypes can trigger aggressive or violent reactions. This is particularly true if the other person is ill at ease because of being in your 'territory', is upset for some reason, has come with feelings of frustration to make a complaint or believes they are set for a battle with bureaucracy in order to have their needs met.

The sorts of behaviour that can trigger aggressive or violent reactions could include, for example,

- talking down to people;

- patronizing them;

- telling people they are wrong to feel the way they do;

- standing on your official dignity;

- trivializing people's concern, upset, frustration, problem;

- using the wrong form of address or the wrong name;

- using certain words or phrases;

138

- expressing assumptions (for example, women can't understand computers);

- ridicule;

- using organizational jargon.

Think about the way you behave towards other people. Are there things that you do that may trigger unwanted reactions from them? Can you assess your own behaviour or would it be helpful to ask others for feedback about how you are received? Do you ever try to put yourself in the other person's place and imagine what or how they may be feeling so you can gauge appropriate responses?

Empathy

There is a tendency to focus on ourselves in situations that are difficult or threatening because of what our bodies are doing, but it is important and helpful to try to think about the other person too.

If you are working in any environment that involves people, especially one which provides a service, dealing with people's problems or any sort of enforcement, you are likely to face difficult interpersonal situations at some time. When people are upset, annoyed or frustrated they are not necessarily in control of themselves or as rational as normal. If they become violent it is quite possible for the person on the receiving end of their behaviour to make matters worse by becoming annoyed or responding inappropriately. While this is understandable it is not very helpful.

When faced with a violent person, try to avoid becoming irritated or angry yourself by empathizing with the other person. Accept the way they perceive the situation (even if they have the wrong end of the stick), acknowledge their feelings are real (even though they may not be reasonable) and allow that, given their starting point, their behaviour is appropriate; it certainly is to them. In other words, put yourself in their shoes and imagine how you might behave. This is a first step in helping you to start from the same point as the other person. If you can establish what they think, believe has happened, are feeling and so on it can be much easier to understand why they are upset or angry and avoid the personal responses of feeling accused or becoming angry yourself. It means you can avoid approaching the situation feeling that you must defend yourself, prove the other person wrong or win. It should not be a win–lose but a win–win situation. To achieve this you need to be able to acknowledge two different starting points, the aims of the two people and work out a process to achieve a compromise or solution that will satisfy (not necessarily totally) both parties.

Unfortunately, many situations degenerate into lose–lose situations of violence where all parties end up dissatisfied or hurt because no one thinks about trying to see the situation from the other side: they are too busy reacting.

Signs and Signals

Someone who is potentially violent can give off signs and signals that constitute a recognizable warning. If you are out and about travelling there are some very obvious warning signs that should alert you to possible danger; for example if people are:

- following you;

- lurking in corners;

- shouting out at you;

- making comments;

- high on drink or drugs;

- staring at you;

- trying to catch your eye;

- trying to make conversation.

In circumstances where you are actually interacting with other people you should look for signs that indicate potential or impending violence such as:

- agitation;

- tapping the table;

- loud speech/shouting;

- muscle tension in face, hands, limbs;

- fidgeting, hand wringing;

- clenching fists;

- drawing breath in sharply;

- colour of face – pale is dangerous: the body is ready for action; red is likely to indicate a bark worse than bite but it could change;

- finger wagging or jabbing;

- inability to be still, even pacing about;

- swearing;

- staring eyes;

- sweating;

- oversensitivity to ideas, suggestions;

- rapid mood swings.

When assessing the risk of violence in a situation you are in or about to enter ask yourself questions, such as:

- Does the person have

    - a history of violence?
    - criminal convictions for violence?
    - a history of psychiatric illness causing violence?
    - a medical condition which may result in loss of self-control?

- Has the person

    - verbally abused me in the past?
    - threatened me with violence before?
    - attacked me before?
    - abused, threatened or attacked colleagues before?

- Is the person likely

    - to be dealing with high levels of stress?
    - to be drunk?
    - to be on drugs?

- Could the person see me as a threat

    - to their liberty?
    - to their family?
    - to them personally?
    - to their business or work?
    - to them getting what they want?

- Has the person got

    - realistic and reasonable expectations of what I can do for them?
    - an impression of me as unhelpful or unwilling?

Ask also:

- do I feel confident to handle the situation?

- have I got back-up?

- can I summon help?

- have I got a plan of how to approach the situation?

AWARENESS OF THE ENVIRONMENT

Being aware of the environment can help you recognize potential risks and ways of avoiding them. To do this you need to take positive and active notice of your surroundings. Environment here means the physical environment around you in the workplace, travelling on business or working in others' homes and premises, and the nature of the business within which you work. Taking notice of your physical environment means taking notice of what and who is around you, including:

- Access – who can get in, where and how?

- Egress – how can you get out? Exits, escape routes, routes to well lit or populated areas.

- Isolation – can you make contact with others, see them or be seen?

- Alarms – how can you raise an alarm or summon help?

- Lighting – at night especially – is your route, car park, meeting place and so on well lit?

- Hiding places – are there corners or places not properly visible or badly lit where people could hide?

- Situations – are you likely to be affected by pub closing time, football crowds or other situations when you may be more at risk?

- Locations – are you conscious of areas of higher risk in the town or city or particularly risky locations such as gardens, parks, underpasses, alleyways and so on?

- Weapons – are there things around you that could be used as weapons by others or present danger?

141

- Precautions – are you aware of the physical forms of protection available to you, and do you or could you use them properly?

- People – do you take notice of other people around you, where they are and what they are doing so that you could recognize risk such as being followed or watched?

Awareness of the nature of the business you work in means being conscious of what it is you do and the risks inherent in it, for example:

- Is there general public access to your place of work?

- Do you have a job which requires you to deal directly with the public?

- Are the public you may deal with likely to present problems because of the purpose of their visit, such as complaints?

- Are you likely to be exposed to people who present a risk because they are ill, drunk or on drugs – for example, in a hospital, social services, police force or probation service?

- Does your work involve you in tasks that may not be popular or lead to a disagreement such as inspection or enforcement (for example, trading standards, environmental health, building inspection)?

- Are you potentially a target because you transport or collect money or valuables?

- Are you employed directly to provide a security service?

- Does your job mean you have to work in others' homes or premises where you may be more or less welcome?

- Do you travel on business or work away from a base and thus become isolated?

Awareness of the working environment is the key to spotting risks and possible danger so that these can then be minimized by adopting safe working practices.

TWO

LINES

2

AINERS

1

Gower Publishing
Gower House
Croft Road
ALDERSHOT
Hampshire
United Kingdom
GU11 3BR

Postcode...........

If you do not wish to receive
information from other

THE TRAINER'S ROLE

When organizations, and trainers within them, embark on training programmes it is not uncommon to discover that the roles of different people in ensuring that the training is effective have been assumed rather than defined. At worst there can be great confusion about who is responsible for what so that learners, full of enthusiasm and expectations, find themselves unable to apply their learning because the support, organizational changes, finance and so forth are not in place.

Investing some time in ensuring there is clarity about and agreement to the role of different people in the organization will certainly bear dividends. If, for example, policy makers and managers are unprepared to accept their role in financing the changes necessary to ensure safe working, is it worth raising expectations through training? If supervisors are not willing to support the development and maintenance of safer working practices can any training be effective? Clarity about the role of various people in ensuring safe working is an essential precursor to ensuring their commitment, which is itself essential if the training is to achieve its aim.

Trainers' roles often encompass an enormous range of tasks and it is not unusual to find that other people impose their expectations on the trainers. It is important to be clear about what is, and what is not, the trainer's role and responsibility and what can reasonably be expected of him/her. You may find it helpful to consider the following areas in determining your role as a trainer, in negotiating that role with others or in communicating your role to others.

- Expertise

  - Are you an expert in the subject?
  - Do you need to be an expert?
  - To what extent do you need to be conversant with the subject?
  - Do you need expert help or input to assist you?
  - Are you an expert trainer?
  - What is your particular expertise as a trainer and what are your weak points?
  - Should you do things you are not confident about?
  - Do you see yourself as an expert or an enabler of learning?
  - Do you know your own limits so as not to put yourself or others at risk?

- Responsibility

  - What can you reasonably be expected to be responsible for – for example, planning, designing, implementing and evaluating the training?
  - What are you not responsible for – for example, policy development, financial decisions, solving the organization's or other people's problems?

- Negotiating

  - Is it your job to negotiate with managers/policy makers for the training to take place, for resources to do it, and to ensure organizational support and commitment?
  - Do you need to negotiate your role with a co-trainer and agree tasks and responsibilities?
  - Do you have a role with other departments, for example, Personnel, to negotiate the implementation of outcomes from the training?

- Communication

  - What should you be communicating and to whom, for example, information about the need for training to policy makers/managers, or to staff in general; information about the training, its aims and objectives to potential learners and your role in it; details of outcomes from the training so that actions can be taken?

- Liaison

    – To what extent is it your role to liaise, for example, with personnel staff on the development of policy, practices and procedures; with policy makers and managers to keep safety issues on their agenda and ensure continued commitment; with health and safety representatives in the workplace to develop their role?

- Monitoring

    – Do you/should you have a part to play in monitoring the effectiveness of practices and procedures?
    – Will you be monitoring and evaluating the effectiveness of the training? – if so, how?

- Advice

    – What sort of advice can you safely provide?
    – Are you responsible for obtaining 'expert' advice?
    – What sort of specialist advice might you need?

VALUES AND BELIEFS

Whether we recognize it consciously or not, all of us operate from a basis of our values and beliefs and this influences our role as trainers. Our own values and beliefs, as well as those underlying materials and resources we use, will have an impact on the training and the learners.

Only you can describe your values and beliefs and those of the organizations in which you work, and it is up to you to explore how they may affect your role as a trainer and the training itself.

The values and beliefs identified here in respect of safety at work and training people are those which underlie this package. They influence its content, style and expectations of how it should be used by trainers.

- Working towards safety is 'our' problem in the sense that everyone has a responsibility. It should never be a 'them' and 'us' situation where management are in confrontation with the workforce or unions. To achieve a safe working environment everyone must play their part.

- People have a right to be safe at work and managers have a duty in law to ensure they are, as far as possible, safe. Equally managers have a right to expect support and cooperation and the workforce has a responsibility to fulfil these expectations.

- Trainers train and learners learn. No matter how good a trainer you are you cannot learn for people; you can only enable their learning. Thus learners have a responsibility to play their part in the learning process.

- Training is most effective when it is learner-centred. That is, the learner's needs, level of experience, preferred style of learning, existing knowledge and working context are all taken into account in designing and providing the training.

- Trainers are enablers of learning. That is, they are a resource, people with expertise and experience (not necessarily an expert on content) in designing and providing learning opportunities.

- Training should be safe for people, especially those who come to training events carrying with them images of school or who are fearful of being challenged, questioned or showing themselves up. Even otherwise confident people can find the new or unusual setting of a training event disconcerting. This is particularly important where the content of the training, as in this case, may evoke emotional responses. Trainers have a role in ensuring the training environment is safe by being clear about its purpose, ground rules and norms of behaviour. It also means trainers may need to support individual learners in difficulty or deal with any inappropriate behaviour.

- Equality is a fundamental consideration throughout training; it should be taken into account in all aspects of the process, for example:

  - range of food to meet all dietary requirements;
  - accessibility for people with disabilities;
  - services such as brailling or induction loops;
  - resources that are free of racist or sexist language;
  - resources that present positive rather than stereotypical images;
  - timing of training so as to take account of the care responsibilities of the group;
  - provision of a creche or child care;
  - dates that do not clash with religious or other festivals, or school holidays;
  - language used should not promote stereotypes, for example, referring to a manager as 'he';
  - not making assumptions about people but checking how they wish to be referred to, for example women or ladies; black people or Asian people;
  - staff in a training venue should know what behaviour is expected of them;
  - venues themselves should not promote stereotypical images, for example pin-ups on the wall;
  - the venue should be safe, that is, have safe, lighted car parks, be secure at night if people are staying, and have transport to and from it if needed;
  - everyone should have the opportunity to express views and opinions and these should be respected.

- Recognizing and using the experience of the learners is important because it

  - involves them actively in the learning;
  - recognizes the value of their experience and builds on it;
  - can increase the perceived relevance of training to individuals;
  - enables learning from each other in the group thus helping group development;
  - is generally what people learn most from, so plan activities for people to experience.

- Training should be constructive and not destructive. The training should not become an opportunity to criticize or a griping session; this may well be cathartic for the group but is unlikely to help in gaining their commitment to change or recognition of their responsibilities within the process.

- In the context of this training about violence it is important to stress that it is not personal but work-related. The training, while being sensitive to people's experience and feelings, is not a counselling activity but is about the work setting and the development of safe working practices.

147

ADULT LEARNERS

As well as having gone through the education system and been at work, adult learners will have considerable life experience. They will have their own values and beliefs; they will have formed their own views and opinions; they will have aspirations and expectations of life and work; they have their own different motivations for doing things and, generally, have a sense of their individuality and individual needs.

When it comes to training, adults often feel their learning ability is not what it was. Sometimes they have unpleasant memories of school or other training; they may fear loss of status or embarrassment if they cannot immediately cope or compete in the learning situation and are often apprehensive of a new situation and new people. They will also want to be sure of the relevance of the training and that it is worth giving time to.

Research demonstrates that the rate of learning in some adults may decline with age, just as memory generally reduces in efficiency as we get older but experience and motivation combined with well designed training can compensate for this.

Bearing all these things in mind the following points may help you in designing and providing training for adult learners.

- Adults will feel more secure if they know where they are being led and how. Explain the aims and objectives of the training, your role as an enabler and supporter of learning and their responsibility as the learners to do the learning but in a setting that you will ensure is as safe and unthreatening as possible.

- Acknowledge their experience and design ways for them to contribute different ideas, views, opinions and suggestions constructively rather than taking an adversary stance and arguing. This requires time in the programme, so plan for it.

- Establish at the start that it is quite normal to feel strange and apprehensive; just knowing that someone else feels the same way can help. Our ability to learn is impaired when emotions such as distress or fear get in the way. It is important that trainers recognize the signs of such emotions and deal with them rather than ignore them.

- Find an introductory exercise that helps people to share their concerns about the training itself.

- Try to establish group norms so that differences are respected and people feel able to express their views, feelings and so on.

- Keep competitiveness to a minimum. Use activities that require cooperation, not competition.

- Use the experience of the group as well as encouragement and praise to boost confidence – but beware of patronizing.

- Design training to move from the concrete to the abstract, from the easy to the difficult. Going step by step, learning one thing and building on it allows people to achieve and grow in confidence. It is also much easier to learn since few of us can launch into a new subject at the abstract level.

- We all learn and remember through our senses. Research into learning and memory shows that we remember

    10 per cent of what we hear
    50 per cent of what we hear and see
    90 per cent of what we hear, see and do

Given this, training designed to stimulate or utilize more than one of the senses at the same time is more likely to be effective in terms of people's learning and retention of it.

- Remembering is also aided by reinforcing what has been learnt with reviews, revision, summaries and plenty of practise.

- Do not be surprised if adults don't accept what you say, argue with you, want to change your programme or raise unexpected issues. Try to be as flexible as you can so that you are meeting individuals' needs but this has to be balanced with meeting the needs of the rest of the group, and achieving the aims and objectives of the training.

- Always link training activities and what people are learning to the work context. This helps to demonstrate relevance and usefulness in a practical way and encourages learning.

IDENTIFYING TRAINING NEEDS

Most trainers will recognize the classic definition of a training need as the gap that exists between the current skills, knowledge, experience, performance, attitudes or behaviour and what is required or desired to do the job now, or in the future, in the organization.

Identifying training needs in relation to safety at work is similar to identifying other needs in that they may

- be general organization-wide needs as a result of policy or practice;

- be needs specific to a group of staff who have particular roles or tasks;

- arise as a result of statutory requirements;

- result from previous problems that demonstrate a need for training;

- have been identified by individuals themselves, supervisors or managers;

- result from the observation of, research into or learning about good practice elsewhere.

It is especially important when identifying needs in this area to be sure that the learners themselves share your perception of the need. You will require their commitment to learning and implementing what they learn and will only obtain that if they perceive a need for it, its relevance to their work and its benefits to them as individuals. In order to achieve this you should consider:

- involving the learners as much as possible in defining their own needs;

- taking time to ensure that, where needs are 'imposed', for example because of statutory or policy requirements, the learners know why these requirements exist and how they are relevant to them and benefit them;

- trying, where the learner's perception of needs goes rather beyond your definition, to accommodate them where appropriate without losing sight of your purpose;

- communicating clearly to people what the needs for particular training are, how you know these needs exist and how the training is designed to meet them;

149

- being as precise as possible about needs: statements such as 'all staff need to be aware of . . .' does not tell people very much. 'All staff are required under their contract and the policy to implement X, Y and Z procedures as described' tells people precisely where the need comes from;

- using a variety of methods to identify needs; you'll get a much more realistic picture;

- not assuming that needs remain static, or stay met! As things change and develop needs will arise so you must keep identifying and meeting them.

AIMS AND LEARNING OBJECTIVES

An aim is an overall statement of the purpose of the training; it describes in broad terms the intentions of the trainer in providing the training. For example, 'the aim of the training event is to introduce participants to the safety policy and their role in implementing it' or 'the training course is designed to ensure all reception staff can operate the new security procedures'.

A learning objective is a much more detailed statement of what will be learned by individuals if the training is completely successful. There are five principles in writing learning objectives:

1. They should always be written with the focus on the learner.

2. They involve making statements about observable behaviour.

3. They define the specific area in which learning will be applied.

4. They should state the acceptable standard of performance.

5. They should state the conditions under which the new behaviour can be displayed.

Simply, this means that learning objectives state what the learner will be able to do, to what standard and under what conditions. For example, the numbers in what follows show how each of the principles is incorporated in the learning objective:

The reception staff (1) will be able to demonstrate each step (2) in the front desk security procedure (3) fully and correctly (4) without assistance from a supervisor (5).

Writing learning objectives is not always easy, especially where what is being learnt is not readily measurable or assessable. The process is easier if you avoid words like 'know', 'appreciate', 'comprehend', 'be familiar with', 'realize', 'understand'. These words describe things that are far from observable (principle 3). You cannot see a person 'appreciate' something or assess to what extent they 'realize' something unless they *act* or *behave* in a way that shows you.

More useful words include 'state', 'describe', 'explain', 'demonstrate', 'identify', 'list', 'prioritize', 'solve', 'perform', 'operate' because these words specify actions you can see and assess. Writing aims and objectives for training and learning may seem time consuming but it is very useful because:

- it helps you, the trainer, to clarify the purpose of the training and the outcomes in terms of what the learners will learn;

150

- the discipline of writing them down, even if it takes time at the beginning, saves time later in identifying appropriate resources and activities;

- they provide a basis for evaluation, something against which to measure success;

- clear aims and objectives make communication about the training much easier, whether you are 'selling' the idea to policy makers and managers or using them to 'market' the training to potential learners;

- aims and objectives not only show the 'destination' of the training but map out the 'route' you will take to get there. This can ensure you and the learners have clarity about and confidence in the process.

MOTIVATING LEARNERS

If people are motivated to learn they are much more likely to learn more readily, perform well and enjoy the process of learning. Generally people are motivated to learn if they are interested, curious, can see personal progress, achievement, reward or added responsibility as a result of learning.

If your design and implementation of training attracts and holds attention, arouses interest and curiosity and is relevant to the learners in terms of the personal benefits they perceive it will have for them, you will have helped to motivate them.

Aspects to consider when designing training include the following:

- Realism – make the learning experience real: let them see, do, feel, hear as much as possible in the process.

- Curiosity – design learning as a puzzle or a problem-solving process and encourage them to seek solutions.

- Variety – beware of boredom! Vary the pace, use several methods and aids and encourage participation and activity.

- Incentives – always ensure people understand *why* they are learning something; ensure they are aware of its relevance and benefit to them, their job, their future.

- Achievement – stress the progress that the learners are making: re-cap what has been learnt to demonstrate their progress to them; congratulate and provide opportunities to 'show off' new-found skills and knowledge.

- Environment – ensure the environment is as pleasant and relaxed as possible, that people's needs for comfort are met (fresh air, warmth, drinks, meals and so on) and that interruptions and distractions are avoided.

- Enthusiasm – you must be enthusiastic and interested or your learners will not be!

- Involvement – wherever possible involve the learners in the process of deciding about the design, content and running of the training. Find out from them what they believe they need and want, and how they would like to learn. Nothing motivates people more than being clear about what they need and want and having confidence that participation in a particular activity will provide it.

151

PLANNING TRAINING

Planning a training event, like planning anything, usually involves making judgements and decisions while taking into account all sorts of complex and interlinked factors. You can simplify the process by posing some basic questions at the outset that will guide you through planning and avoid missing aspects out.

The following checklists, although *not exhaustive*, pose some key questions in planning.

- What?

    - are the needs that have been identified?
    - is the training intended to achieve, its aims and objectives?
    - is the event – a two-hour session, a week's course?
    - can you realistically achieve in the time?
    - approach is best and is possible in the time?
    - resources do you require (people, funds, equipment, materials)?
    - are you good at, confident doing?
    - help do you need (administrative, specialist input)?

- Who?

    - is the training for (adults, particular group of staff, cross-section of staff)?
    - is responsible for what (for example, bookings, printing materials, briefing people, presenting, evaluation)?
    - do you need to communicate with, for example, co-trainers or contributors to do the planning, participants about arrangements, managers about outcomes of training?
    - is responsible for follow-up action?
    - should be involved in decisions about the training – managers, participants, trainers?
    - are the trainers? Why have they been chosen? What is their particular expertise and experience?

- When?

    - will the training take place? If it is part of a series, does it need to fit in with other things? Will the timing exclude people, for example, parents in school holidays, part-time staff? Does the timing allow for planning, preparation, briefing and so on? Have you checked that others involved can meet your timescale?
    - do people need to have information about the training and their part in it? Do you need to have made particular decisions, secured commitment of others, made bookings and so on?

- Where?

    - will the event take place? Is there a choice about where it is held? Will it be in the workplace or outside – what is preferable and why? (bear in mind interruptions, whether people are contactable). Does the venue meet equal opportunities criteria in terms of access and services? Is the environment appropriate – space, heating, light, comfortable seats, noise, training equipment and facilities?
    - are people travelling from? Is there public transport that can be safely used? Are there parking facilities that are safe?

152

- How?

    - are you (and others perhaps) going to train the participants? What approach you will take?
    - will you involve participants in decisions about the training?
    - will you involve participants in the training itself?
    - will you decide on content, materials, aids, methods to be used? The choice may be influenced by aims and objectives, group size, time available, your trainer skills, the group's preferences, space available and so on.
    - will you evaluate the effectiveness of the training and how will these data inform future training and practice?
    - will the training be followed up, for example, by further training, supporting learners, organizational changes?
    - will you manage difficult people in a group, potentially contentious issues, conflict, a situation where someone gets upset or needs particular help, the group saying 'This is not what we want', demands for management to change practices?

- Why?

    - is the training being planned? Make sure that there is a need for it, that there is support for it in the organization and that there are not unreasonable expectations that the training itself will solve all the problems or automatically bring about change.
    - are you doing the training? Are you the best person to do it? Are you putting yourself or others at risk? Have you secured the help and support you need?

As you answer these and other questions you will be able to produce a training programme for yourself and/or for use by other people. Whatever your programme is for, and however detailed you feel you need to make it, you will probably want to include some or all of the following:

- Aim – a general statement of the purpose of the training.

- Objectives – specific statements describing what the participants will learn and be able to do as a result.

- Target group – who the training is for, why they need it, how they will benefit, how it links to their work or other training.

- Timing – when it will take place: dates and times; remember to show all the times of a series of events.

- Location – where the training will take place: facilities and limitations of the venue, for example access; how to get there; where the rooms to be used are.

- The trainer/s – who will do the training: you, colleagues or outside specialists. Give their names and perhaps some information about them such as background and experience.

- Content – information about the content of the training. For your use you may want a great deal of detail; if it is for use by participants you may just use session headings.

- Approach – a description of the approach to be taken in the training event. If the information is for participants you may just want to say 'the approach will be varied, involving input by trainers and participative activities'. If the programme is for your use you may want to go into much more detail such as outlining how to run an exercise.

- Evaluation – how the effectiveness of the training will be assessed and when, for example,

  - by a questionnaire at the end of the event;
  - by peer or self assessment during training;
  - by assessment back in the workplace.

- Contacts – for your use: names and contact numbers and addresses of people responsible for administration, printing, the venue, transport, catering and so on. For participants' use: your name and how to contact you, perhaps also a contact in case you are not there, how to contact the venue.

When you first start developing plans for training you may need and want to go into great detail. As you become more experienced you will probably find that the process becomes easier and also that it is quicker because you are confident with less detail. No matter how thoroughly and carefully you plan, the chances are that things will not go exactly to plan all the time. Your plan will need to be flexible because you cannot predict how a group will respond or contribute. In a sense you need to plan for the unpredictable! Obviously, therefore, it is not wise to be determined to see your plan through, come what may, simply because it is THE plan.

In developing your plan try to produce something that can be adapted, depending on the group's response, but will still achieve your purposes. For example, you may plan to use a roleplay to help people learn about behaviour that calms or heightens aggression. If the group flatly refuses to do a roleplay you need to have another method 'up your sleeve' such as a brainstorm under the heading of 'heightens aggression' and 'calms aggression'; or divide into two sub-groups and ask each group to come up with a list of behaviours under those headings.

Ways of overcoming resistance to your plan are to develop it with the group, and to share it with the group at the start, get their views, make changes if necessary – agree a plan everyone owns.

PRESENTING TRAINING

If you ask any experienced trainer he/she will tell you that the only way to learn about presenting training is by doing it. What you learn most from is the experience and the development of an 'extra sense' that comes from that. Like driving, it needs plenty of practice; after all few of us are really good at driving when we first pass our tests and get a licence. However, as with driving, you need to stick to some basic principles and develop competent practice before you start, so that you and other people are safe.

Before you attempt to present any training you should have planned it, designed it and got together the resources you will need. You should know from your plan what you propose to do, when and how. Even the most experienced trainers benefit from the discipline of preparing a plan and find it useful support and guidance during training.

Remember, though, the need to be flexible and adapt your plan in response to the learners' needs, preferences and responses. This is where experience comes in.

The most perfectly planned training can be wasted if the presentation is poor. You can minimize the risk of this by designing each session so that it develops logically and fits in with what has gone before and what is to follow.

Think of a training session as being like a book or a meal, with a beginning, a middle and an end, and each part having a particular purpose. To do justice to the subject of presenting training is beyond the scope of this package; what follows is a brief guide to key points.

Beginning

The purpose of the beginning is to gain attention, arouse curiosity and stimulate the desire to learn. INTRO is a mnemonic to help you remember the sorts of things to include in the beginning, though not necessarily in the order shown.

I – Interest. You need to find ways to create interest. You could introduce yourself and get learners to introduce themselves – use a short ice-breaker exercise to get involvement early on in an event. At the start of a new session do a warm up exercise, or tell them what is coming up.

N – Need. Make sure the learners know early on how the training will meet their needs; explain how it will help them and how it is relevant to their work.

T – Title. Tell the learners what the training is about; it may or may not have a self-explanatory title.

R – Range. Let the learners know early on the range of the subject to ensure they have realistic expectations of what will be learnt. You could give them a programme or timetable and talk them through it.

O – Objectives. Explaining the learning objectives will help make sure the learners will know what is expected of them, and what they will be able to do at the end of the process.

This is a guide to what you can include in the beginning; how you mix individual items will depend on the subject, the situation, the scope of the training and the particular learners. As a rough guide the beginning should take about 10 per cent of the total time of the session.

Middle

This is the main part of the session and may include a range of activities depending on the situation. You should present material logically, step by step. Make sure everyone has understood before moving from one step to the next. Make links to other parts of the session where appropriate, reminding learners of earlier points to help reinforce the learning. Encourage the learners to participate, question or seek further explanation or clarification if it is needed.

Try to vary the pace and use a variety of methods if time permits; this helps retain attention and interest. Take breaks; in long sessions, the average length of time most people can concentrate hard for is only 20 minutes.

Keep the presentation logical; it is usually best to present material going from:

known	→	unknown
easy	→	difficult
concrete	→	abstract

Few of us can deal with new, complicated or abstract ideas instantly; we need to build on a firm foundation of what we already know and can do.

155

Confirm learning at each step, go over it again if there is confusion, and congratulate the learners as they learn, to encourage them and give them confidence.

The middle part of a session should normally take up about 80 per cent of the total time.

End

The end part of a session may include:

- confirmation of what has been learnt;

- an opportunity for learners to confirm or clarify points;

- a summary of all the key points from the training session;

- a look forward to the next part of the training;

- some form of evaluation;

- confirmation of how the learning from this event fits into the world of the learners;

- a closing activity or exercise.

This part of the training should be about 10 per cent of the total time. While it is important to finish on time – people may have plans – it is also helpful to be available in case individual learners have queries, problems, questions or grumbles that are best dealt with as soon as possible.

TRAINING AIDS

A training aid is intended to add to the training, make it clearer or easier to understand and remember. If an aid is to be useful it needs to be taken seriously and time given to its preparation.

A training aid can be any number of things from the very simple (a blackboard) to the very complex (a three-dimensional working model). Each aid will have advantages and disadvantages, making it more or less appropriate for use in specific circumstances. It is important to remember that training aids should be exactly that – aids. You cannot escape your responsibilities as a trainer by showing films or using elaborately prepared overhead transparencies without using them in the context of carefully planned training. An aid can only support you – adding to the training, not doing it for you.

The following checklists may help you in choosing and using training aids. First, when choosing a training aid consider:

- Cost – can you justify the expenditure in relation to what it will achieve? Could the time/money spent on it be used more effectively?

- Practicality – only use material or equipment you are sure it is practical to use, for example, power is available if required; there is space to use it; it can be seen or heard in the room.

156

- Confidence – only use something you are sure you can use properly, and effectively; otherwise it will cause problems and distractions. Or get help from someone who can use it if you feel it is essential.

- Safety – make sure you can use aids or equipment safely: check fixings, voltage, plugs, avoid trailing wires or things that may fall.

- Concentration – avoid 'gimmicky' aids or aids that are too clever; they can detract from the training rather than adding to it because the learners become more interested in the aid than the message.

When using a training aid remember:

- Prepare the aids properly; badly prepared aids are more hindrance than help.

- Practise using aids beforehand so that you are confident with them and they add to the training rather than distract people.

- Make sure the aids are really necessary because they increase clarity, understanding or remembering – don't use them because they are available or to prove you can.

- Keep aids simple; otherwise they may go wrong, confuse or distract people.

- Make sure aids are large enough or loud enough so that people do not have to strain their eyes or ears.

- Once you have used it, remove it, so as not to create a distraction.

- Aids should be interesting and command attention, stimulate interest or trigger discussion.

- Aids should enhance what you say, not repeat it unless they are specifically for the purpose of reviewing or summarizing.

TRAINING METHODS

There are very many different training methods as well as adaptations to each particular method. Some methods are straightforward, requiring little planning and time and few resources. Others are more complex, time-consuming, need a great deal of careful planning and a range of resources. Whatever method you select it is important to remember to:

- Plan it – know why and how you are going to use it and what learning should result.

- Make sure you have all the resources you need properly organized and to hand, including space.

- Allow time to use the method properly and time to 'process' it: review it, discuss it, analyse it and extract the learning points from it. You need at least as much time to process as to run an activity.

- Make sure the learners know why you are suggesting they undertake particular activities, and what the outcome will be.

- Make sure you use the method well: practise if you can; be sure you know what instructions to give, the order of events and so on.

- If a method is likely to arouse feelings and emotions you must be confident that you can deal with them and help learners to understand what has happened, why and how to learn from it.

- If you are not sure you can deal with the possible results of using a particular method, do *not* use it.

- Select methods because they are appropriate and will achieve the learning you want to achieve not because they are complex or fancy. The simplest of methods is often the most effective.

- If learners really do not want, or are afraid, to get involved in particular activities, do not force them. Forcing people into activities they are afraid of, embarrassed about or feel they cannot cope with may put them off training altogether. They will certainly not learn very much from something they have to do against their will.

- Methods that are fun and create laughter and excitement can be very effective; however, you need to be sure you can manage the activity so that people do learn and so that calm can be restored afterwards.

- Try not to stick to a very few methods you find easy or safe with because

  - using a variety of methods helps sustain interest and attention by varying the pace and level of activity of the learners;
  - the same method used for long periods loses its effect and becomes boring;
  - you will not develop your range of skills;
  - you may become bored doing the same thing over and over again and convey your boredom to learners.

- Select methods that are appropriate to the stage of development of the group. For example, do not try to use methods requiring much self-disclosure if the group members do not know each other or do not have confidence in each other.

- Select methods appropriate to the time of day. For example, use methods involving learners in activity after lunch, the so-called 'graveyard session' when they may feel like a nap and are likely to take one if you lecture to them!

- No matter how well a method is described to you, in a book or by other trainers, there is no substitute for experience. If possible try

  - to use the method as a co-trainer at first with an experienced colleague;
  - to ask colleagues or friends to be 'guinea pigs' and allow you to practise the method on them;
  - if all else fails – to practise by yourself.

All the preparation and practice in the world will not ensure that the methods you choose will work for every group, every time. If a method does not work as well as you would wish, try to work out why. For example:

- Did you do something wrong?

- Did you leave something out?

- Was it really the most appropriate method for the purpose?

- Were you clear enough about why you used it?

- Did that particular group simply not like the method?

- Was there some external factor you could not control such as noise or interruptions?

Whatever the answer, you can learn from experience and use that to develop your skills in using a variety of methods.

EVALUATING TRAINING

Evaluation processes are generally used to obtain information about the results of training. This information is then used to assess the value and effectiveness of the training with a view to improving it if necessary. Evaluation is an important part of the training process because

- it helps to show whether the aims and objectives of the training have been achieved;

- it can demonstrate that the training has been effective by showing how the learning has resulted in changed behaviour or practice, or changes in the quality of service;

- it can highlight ways in which the training could be made more effective;

- it may provide evidence to support choices already made in relation to the design, timing, style, content and so on of the training;

- it can provide information on which to base decisions about further or future training;

- it may highlight problems, difficulties or further needs the learners have;

- it is a means of assessing the relevance and appropriateness of the training for particular groups of staff (for example women, front-line staff) or people undertaking particular roles or tasks (staff making home visits, interviewers);

- it can be used to test one method or way of doing things against others;

- it may indicate where resources are lacking or used uneconomically;

- it can be used to demonstrate 'value' in relation to resources required such as money, time, space, materials, personnel;

- it can be used to demonstrate to those who supported, took part in or contributed to the training that their efforts were worthwhile.

Evaluating training is much easier if you have set clear aims and objectives in the first place. These provide you with something against which you can measure or assess achievement. They will also help you to identify the sort of information you require from the evaluation process because they define what you set out to achieve.

There are many ways of obtaining information for evaluation purposes. Here are some examples:

- Use a questionnaire at the end of a session, event or programme to obtain immediate reactions.

- Use a questionnaire some weeks or months after the training to help assess if learning has been remembered and/or used in the workplace.

- Design an exercise during, or after, the training to collect information. For example, invite people to write comments under appropriate headings on pieces of flip-chart paper pinned around the room – this is called the 'graffiti exercise'.

- Ask learners to comment verbally at the end of the training on its value and record their responses.

- Visit learners at the workplace some time after the training and interview (structured or unstructured) them to obtain comments.

- Talk with the line managers of the learners after the event to get their views on how the learner has developed.

- Ask learners to write to you some time after the event with their views at this later time – compare this with the views immediately after the event.

- Bring the group back together and hold an evaluation session, asking them to comment on the particular aspects you need information about.

- Ask learners to keep a diary for an agreed time after the training and record when/if and how they used the learning.

These are just a few ideas of how you could go about collecting evaluation data. There are many other methods, some very complex, that you could learn and you can of course invent your own.

The most important thing to remember is that there is no point in evaluating unless you are prepared to take note of the findings and make any necessary changes, even if this means admitting mistakes, poor decisions or performance and errors of judgement.

PART THREE

SAMPLE TRAINING PROGRAMMES

INTRODUCTION TO VIOLENCE AT WORK

Aim

Notes for trainers

To increase awareness of the problem of violence at work and how to keep safe.

This is a very short introductory programme and is very simple, but designed to mean that each participant can take some action afterwards.

Objectives

At the end of the programme the participants will be able to:
– say what is meant by violence at work;
– identify risks they may face at work;
– describe actions they will take to ensure safety at work.

Time

2½ hours

Target Group

All staff to whom the subject of violence at work and keeping safe needs to be introduced. This programme could also be included in a general health and safety programme.

A small group will work best in this short time if people are to participate – 12–16 people.

Resources

Flipcharts and stand, pens, any pre-prepared materials or handouts.

Environment

A room large enough for the whole group to sit comfortably in a circle and for people to split up to work in pairs for a short time.

163

Timetable

1. Introduction   15 mins   *Timings are*
2. What do we mean by violence at work?   30 mins   *approximate.*
3. Minimizing risk   60 mins
4. Safer practice – personal action plan   30 mins
5. Summary/evaluation   15 mins

Contents

1. Introduction

- Introduce yourself and the training programme saying what the aims and objectives are.

- Ask the group members to introduce themselves.   *You could use a simple introductory exercise or just ask for names.*

- Give any 'housekeeping' information such as time you will finish, where toilets are, etc.

2. What do we mean by violence at work?

- Gather the group's ideas of what violence at work is.   *See Part One Chapter 1. Brainstorming is a simple method that could be used to do this.*

- Discuss what they would include in the term 'violence at work' and what they would exclude and why.

- Explain to or show the group how other people define violence at work.   *Pre-prepare an OHP or flipchart with the definitions on pp. 12–14.*

- Ensure the group understand violence is used as an all-embracing term to cover a range of behaviour and its effects.

3. Minimizing risk

- Identify areas of work you know the group is involved in or familiar with, e.g. reception, travelling, dealing with the public, handling money. Go through each area asking the group to identify risks or potential risks, adding to their ideas if necessary. Record their ideas on a flip chart.   *Identifying Risks at Work – see Part One Chapter 4 and Workwise Part One Chapter 10.*

- Go back through each of the areas and the risks identified in it asking the group to suggest actions that could be taken to reduce the risks or to avoid it altogether. Add to the groups suggestions if needed.   *You could give a list of areas to pairs and ask them to record their initial ideas on risks and then share with the group. Or assign one area of work to a pair and ask them to draw up an initial list and then, with the group, add to it.*

- Decide with the group which of the actions they have identified can be taken by them individually or as a group, and which need management agreement and support or the support of others. Record this.

4. Safer practice – personal action plan

- Individuals prepare a personal action plan listing actions they   *Individuals can work* can take independently to minimize the risks they face and any actions they can take to bring risks that need action from others to the attention of the appropriate people.

on this alone or in pairs or trios to help each other.

- As the group complete action plans ask them to look through them again and put deadlines on their actions where possible; this will encourage them to stick to their decisions.

You could also prepare a proforma action plan for them to complete.

5. Summary/evaluation

- Summary – go back over the key learning points:

    - what we mean by violence at work;
    - areas of risk identified;
    - ideas for minimizing risks;
    - actions people have decided to take.

You could quote some examples of actions and encourage the group to follow up with each other to see how well they stick to their plans.

- Evaluation: either

    - conduct a brief evaluation on the content and conduct of the programme, venue etc., or
    - explain how the programme will be evaluated later.

A simple form or group evaluation will be all there is time for within the programme.

THE MANAGER'S ROLE IN PREVENTING VIOLENCE AT WORK – AN INTRODUCTION

Aim

To ensure managers are aware of their duties and roles in ensuring the safety of employees at work.

Notes for trainers

This is an introductory programme so covers a range of topics without going into great depth.

Objectives

At the end of the programme participants will be able to:

- explain their duties as employers in respect of employee safety;

- identify why action in the workplace on safety is necessary;

- prepare an action plan for themselves to assist in developing safety measures.

Time

3¹/₂ hours

Target Group/s

Managers, specifically those whose roles involve them in policy development and implementation who have had no prior training in managing violence at work.

In some situations board members, or similar policy makers such as councillors, could be involved. Group size limited by number that can participate – more than 20 is unmanageable.

Resources

OHP and/or flipchart and pens. Any pre-prepared materials or handouts.

Environment

A room large enough for the group with space to work in sub-groups. An area for break time.

Timetable

1. Introduction	15 mins
2. Defining violence at work	15 mins
3. Employer duties and the need for action	1 hour
BREAK	15 mins
4. Taking steps to safety	1 hour
5. Action planning	30 mins
6. Summary/evaluation	15 mins

Contents

1. Introduction

- Introduce yourself and the training programme using the aims and objectives.

- Ask group members to introduce themselves.

  It may be worthwhile asking them to identify the role they feel they have in ensuring safety.

- Give any housekeeping information such as break time, finishing time.

2. Defining violence at work – a brief input session

  See Part One, Chapter 1.

- Explain 'violence' is used in a broad sense, encompassing a wide range of behaviour and the effects of it.

  Answer questions or queries but avoid detailed discussion.

- Using pre-prepared OHP slides or flipchart show them definitions used by others – or develop your own to show them.

- Identify for the group why having a definition of violence at work is useful and important.

  You may want to ask the group why they think a definition is important but this will take longer and needs planning for.

3. Employer duties and the need for action

  See Part One, Chapter 3.

- Ask the group what they believe to be the legal duties of an employer to ensure safety.

- Using pre-prepared handouts, OHP slides or flipchart show the group a list of their duties under Health and Safety at Work Act and common law and the risks of civil actions against them. Compare with their list – how accurate are they?

  A handout of employer duties will be a useful item to take away – use pp. 30–31 to develop.

- Ask the group what they believe the consequences of not taking action to ensure employee safety are:

  - in legal terms;
  - in terms of the effects on the organization.

  See Part One, Chapter 3, p. 31.

168

Record responses on flipchart or OHP – offer ideas or add things they miss.

BREAK – 15 mins

4. Taking steps to safety

See Part One, Chapter 3, p. 33.

- Explain the Health and Safety Executive booklet *Preventing Violence to Staff* proposes a 7-step action plan for combating violence at work and what the steps are – write them up on the flipchart or OHP beforehand.

- Go through each step with the group explaining what it involves and why it is important. Ask for the group's views on how (or whether) they could take each of the steps. Do they feel it is a useful approach?
  Can they add suggestions or ideas for their own organization/s?

Another approach would be to give sub-groups a copy of the 7 steps to read, discuss and record their views, reaction and ideas. They could then return to the whole group to share results.

5. Action planning

- The action plans should describe actions that will be taken; by whom or who will be responsible for seeing they are taken and the timescales.

- The actions could range from a management meeting to discuss combating violence at work to hiring a consultant to investigate risks and make proposals.

- The action plans should be achievable and people encouraged to follow up with each other to check on progress.

It the group are all from one organization they could develop an action plan together for the organization with your help to manage the process. If there are sub-groups from a number of organizations they could work in those sub-groups on the action plan.

6. Summary/Evaluation

- Summary – go back over the key learning points from the programme:
  - a broad definition of violence at work;
  - the need for employers to act to combat violence at work because of their legal obligations and the effects of violence at work on the organization and individuals;
  - action planning;
  - the 7-step approach to an action plan on violence at work;
  - action decided upon by participants.

- Evaluation – conduct a brief evaluation using a form or group activity focussing on key areas such as:
  - most significant learning points;
  - what else they would like to know or do;
  - effectiveness of materials, trainer etc.

Explain what and how further evaluation will be done.

LOOKING AFTER YOURSELF – TENSION AND RELAXATION

Aim

To assist learners in the development of tension control techniques.

Objectives

At the end of the programme learners will be able to:

- identify and describe common causes of tension;
- describe the effects of tension;
- demonstrate relaxation techniques;
- develop a personal action plan.

Time

1 day

Target Groups

All staff

Group size depends upon the space available but a smaller group is best – 10–12 people.

Resources

Flipchart and pens and/or OHP, any materials or handouts including copies of the relaxation exercises.

Environment

A room large enough for the group to spread out, use the floor space. They need to dress very casually, e.g. track suits.

Timetable

1. Introduction	30 mins
2. What we mean by tension	1 hour
BREAK	15 mins
3. Causes of tension – fear, anger and stress	1½ hours
LUNCH	1 hour
4. Taking care of yourself – relaxation	1½ hours
BREAK	15 mins
5. Looking after yourself and managing tension at work	1 hour
6. Action plans	30 mins
7. Summary/evaluation	30 mins

Contents

1. Introduction

- Introduce yourself and the training programme using the aims and objectives to describe the content you will cover and the outcomes.

- Ask the group members to introduce themselves.

- Explain 'housekeeping' arrangements such as break times, meal arrangements, location of facilities etc.

Take time to get the group to introduce themselves using an exercise; it will help them with the rest of the day.

2. What we mean by tension

See Part One, Chapter 8, p. 69.

- Ask the group (or sub-groups you set up) to say what they mean by tension and what physical and other effects they associate with tension – either ask sub-groups to record their ideas or record the ideas from the whole group.

- Using the group's ideas, adding to them if necessary, explain that tension is necessary but constant or excessive tension can be harmful; produce a handout or list on an OHP transparency or flipchart of the possible harmful effects of constant or excessive tension.

Use pp. 70–71.

- Ask the group for examples of situations where they have experienced tension and the effects they felt. Explain that they will be learning ways to defuse or control tension.

Here make sure you manage the time carefully – ask for brief examples.

BREAK – 15 mins

3. Causes of tension – fear, anger and stress

See Part One, Chapter 8.

- Explain that emotions such as fear and anger cause tension as does stress.

- Fear – the group need to know the positive and negative aspects of fear. You could present that information to them or divide the group in two and ask one group to prepare a list of the positive aspects and the other group the negative aspects of fear. Ask each group to explain the points they have made while you and the rest of the group can add to the list until all the points are covered.

   See pp. 63–64.

   With the group discuss the physical effects of fear – they could imagine a time when they were actually afraid and how it felt – and make sure they recognize these effects as tension.

- Anger – try using the example in the text or one you invent as a roleplay. As you review what happened explain how angry situations develop. It should be clear how overt anger leads to violence – ask or explain how repressed anger can also lead to violence. Ask the group to identify situations from their work setting that could/do lead to anger.

   See pp. 64–66.

   See p. 9.

- Stress – explain the need for some stress and the difference between stress and overstress. Ask the group – try using a 'round robin' or 'brainstorm' – what the effects of stress are and make sure they recognize these as tension.

   See pp. 66–67.

   See p. 9.
   See pp. 67–69.

   Prepare a list of the common causes of stress at work as a handout or OHP slide and ask the group (or sub-groups if there is time) to give examples of what causes stress at work under each heading. Explain you will come back to these common causes later and suggest ways of managing them.

BREAK FOR LUNCH – 1 hour

4. Taking care of yourself – relaxation

- Explain to the group that relaxation is an effective approach to controlling tension both in the face of immediate danger (quick relaxation of tension) and longer term (tension control technique).

   See pp. 71–72.

- Explain quick relaxation of tension, what it is for and the rules; stress the need for practice. Either take the whole group through the exercise or divide into pairs: one partner guides the other through the exercise, they then change roles – repeat as often as time allows. Everyone should have a copy of the exercise for practice.

   See pp. 72–73.

- Describe the benefits of longer-term relaxation, what they need to do to learn it and what they need to do before practising the technique. Again either take the group through the tension control technique exercise or divide them into pairs so they can guide each other. Practise as long as time allows.

   See pp. 73–75.

BREAK – 15 mins

5. Look after yourself and managing tension at work

See pp. 75–76.

- Identify for or with the group the practical things they can do to look after themselves.

An activity could be useful here after all the relaxation.

- Refer the group back to the list of the common causes of stress used before lunch. Using the same headings, ask the group to suggest practical things they could do to manage the stress associated with each of these headings. Add to the list/s the group/s generate or give out the list from the text as a handout they can compare with their own list.

See pp. 76–79.

This could be done in sub-groups taking all the headings, or sub-groups concentrating on 3 or 4 headings each.

6. Action plans

- Each person to individually prepare an action plan identifying:
    - what gives rise to tension in them;
    - what actions they are going to take to deal with the causes of tension;
    - what they will do to relax and look after themselves;
    - the deadlines they have set themselves;
    - how they will check on their own progress or get help to do this from others.

- Ask them to explain their action plan to others in pairs or trios so they can clarify points for each other, make suggestions or pose questions. They can amend or add to action plans through this process.

- Encourage group members, especially if they work together, to offer to support each other, check on progress, offer encouragement etc.

7. Summary/evaluation

- Summarize the key learning points from each part of the day either verbally or pre-prepare an OHP, flipchart or handout including
    - what we mean by tension;
    - the effects of tension and possible violent consequences of it;
    - the causes of tension;
    - the importance of relaxation, looking after yourself and managing tension at work.

- Evaluation – design an evaluation, based on a form or exercise, to identify
    - what the group found to be most and least informative, effective, useful, enjoyable etc;
    - what they will be able to use/not use;
    - what they feel could be done differently or kept the same.
    Explain any post-dated evaluation process you would like the group to take part in.

A group exercise evaluation could work well as the group have worked and relaxed together.

COPING WITH VIOLENCE

Aim

To equip staff with basic skills in coping with violent behaviour towards them.

Objectives

At the end of the programme learners will be able to:

- identify a range of violent behaviour;

- describe potential triggers to violent behaviour;

- describe the signs of impending violent behaviour;

- identify a range of actions they could take in the event of being faced with a violent person;

- explain the 'control trilogy' as a process for coping with non-physical violent behaviour.

There is no expectation that they will be able to use the control trilogy effectively without further practice.

Time

1 day initially and follow-up practice sessions.

Target Groups

'Frontline' staff who deal regularly with the public, customers or clients.

Too large a group makes practice difficult; 15 is an ideal number as they can work in trios to do practice roleplays with an observer as described later.

Resources

OHP and/or flipchart and pens, pre-prepared handouts and other materials such as briefs for role-play and observers.

Environment

A room large enough for the group to move off and work in sub-groups or provide syndicate rooms.

175

Timetable

1. Introduction	30 mins
2. What is violent behaviour?	1 hour
BREAK	15 mins
3. Causes and signs of danger	45 mins
4. What to do when faced with violence	1 hour
LUNCH	1 hour
5. The control trilogy	2¼ hours
6. Action plans	30 mins
7. Summary/evaluation	30 mins

Contents

1. Introduction

- Introduce yourself and the training programme using the aims and objectives to explain the content and outcomes.

- Ask the group members to introduce themselves.

- Explain 'housekeeping' arrangements such as meal times, breaks, where facilities are.

A 'warm-up' exercise will help to get the group to know each other and get them participating.

2. What is violent behaviour?

See Part One, Chapter 1.

- Using a simple exercise such as a brainstorm get the group to identify behaviour that is violent.

- Explain that 'violence' is being used to describe a wide range of behaviour (rather than using other words such as aggression, abusive behaviour, rudeness, harassment) of the physical and non-physical type.

- Ask the group if they can now add to the original list of violent behaviour – help them if necessary.

- Using the working definitions of violence if you wish, ensure that the group has a shared understanding of behaviour, and its effects, that constitutes violence.

See pp. 12–14.

BREAK – 15 mins

3. Causes and signs of danger

See Part One, Chapter 13 pp. 138–141.

- Causes of violence – lead a group discussion having posed the question 'why do people become violent?'. The discussion should identify range of possible causes from drunkenness and drug taking to frustration or anger because of poor service.

Notes for trainers

- Identify the most likely causes of violence in the workplace/s of group members.

- Signs of danger – explain to the group that it is both verbal and non-verbal communication that signals impending violence. Verbal threats or suggestions of violence are readily recognized. However, verbal signals are generally much rarer than non-verbal and so recognizing non-verbal signs of danger is important.

See Part One, Chapter 12, pp. 127–134; and Part One, Chapter 13, pp. 139–141.

- Get the group to identify non-verbal signs of danger; this is often most effectively done by asking volunteers to demonstrate anger or frustration by giving them a short roleplay.

- Review the roleplay (or other activity you may use) and either write up a list of the behaviour identified as danger signs or provide the group with a pre-prepared handout based on the text.

4. What to do when faced with violence

- Distinguish between physical and non-physical violence and explain that after lunch they will learn one method that can help in coping with non-physical violence.

See Part One, Chapter 11, pp. 118–122.

NB Stress throughout that they must not feel they have to cope with violence – they must do whatever will keep them safe.

- Physical violence – explain that the options when facing physical attack are
  - getting away;
  - fighting back – fighting free;
  - defusing the situation.

Ask the group how they would get away, fight back or try to defuse the situation. For each use the text to explain good safe practice and to explain why some of the ideas they may have are actually likely to put them at greater risk.

Participants in these sorts of programmes often imagine they could do things like poke people's eyes out or defend themselves with an umbrella – they need to be clear about what is really likely to be possible in the event and what is safe.

- Develop with (or use a pre-prepared handout) the group a list of key points to remember in the event of physical attack.

- Someone is likely to raise the issue of self-defence; ensure they are clear of the pros and cons of learning and attempting to use self defence.

LUNCH – 1 hour

5. The control trilogy

See Part One, Chapter 11, pp. 118–122.

- Introduce the control trilogy as a useful method for helping deal with non-physical violence; make sure the group remember they do not have to try to cope if it is safer not to do so, and that they are clear that the control trilogy should not be assumed to always be appropriate or successful.

- Using the text, and handouts you prepare from it, go through each of the stages – calming, reaching and controlling –

177

explaining its purpose, what it involves, answering questions, discussing points etc.

- Give the group time to read the material you have provided and clarify the points.

- Set up a practice exercise using roleplay outlines you have prepared that are relevant in the group's working environment and allow them to practise the stages of the control trilogy.

    You could also try using case examples the group provide or want to work through.

    Trio exercises work well for this kind of practice with three roles: the violent person, the victim and an observer. Each of the group members (AB+C) gets the chance to play each role. The diagram shows how it works.

	Violent person	Victim	Observer
Time period 1	A	B	C
Time period 2	C	A	B
Time period 3	B	C	A

You need to make clear there are three time periods and they need to be about 20 minutes each. You need to brief the observers on what to look for (i.e. changes in behaviour, what worked or did not etc.).

- Review the exercise picking out key learning points, what the group felt about the method, what worked and did not work, how the group feel they could or would use the method.

BREAK – 15 mins

6. Action plans

- Ask the group to individually prepare an action plan identifying what they will do to implement what they have learnt, e.g.
    - what will they do differently?
    - how will they use what they have learnt to help them recognize danger and cope with possibly violent people?
    - what will they avoid doing?

- With the whole group – or those who wish to do so – work out a timetable for further practice of the control trilogy.

    Some of the group may not feel able or willing to use the method and forcing further practice may not be worthwhile.

7. Summary/evaluation

- Summarize the key learning points from the day either verbally or written up on an OHP, flipchart or handout.

178

Notes for trainers

- Using an evaluation exercise questionnaire ask the group to identify, e.g. what has been:
  - most useful/least useful;
  - well done/not so well done;
  - most enjoyable/least enjoyable;
  - most relevant/least relevant; and

  what they will:
  - use at work/not use;
  - use in their personal life/not use; and

  what they would have liked:
  - more of/less of;
  - to include/to exclude.

- Explain any further evaluation process that you wish to conduct with them.

179

COMMUNICATION SKILLS

Aim

To enable learners to develop communication skills that will help them avoid or cope with violent situations.

Objectives

At the end of the programme learners will be able to:

- describe how self-awareness and the awareness of others contributes to effective communication;

- explain what is meant by 'body language' and its importance in communication;

- explain what is meant by assertiveness;

- demonstrate assertive communications.

Time

1 day

Target Groups

All staff, but particularly those who regularly deal with the public, clients, customers and other colleagues.

Group size needs to be manageable, given the practice sessions in the afternoon.

Resources

OHP and/or flipchart and pens; any pre-prepared materials and handouts (e.g. comparisons of types of behaviour, list of 'rights').

181

Environment

A room large enough for the whole group to split into smaller groups for practice or, preferably, syndicate rooms or further space for practice sessions.

Timetable

1.	Introduction	30 mins
2.	Non-verbal communication	1½ hours
BREAK		15 mins
3.	Assertiveness – introduction	1¼ hours
LUNCH		1 hour
4.	Assertiveness – practice	3¼ hours
5.	Action Plan	15 mins
6.	Summary/evaluation	30 mins

In session 4 include a 15-minute break at an appropriate point. Also remember this is initial practice and will not turn them into experts; they will need further practice.

Contents

1. Introduction

- Introduce yourself.

- Use a brief exercise to enable the participants to introduce themselves.

- Introduce the programme using the aims and objectives to describe the content and outcomes.

- Explain any 'housekeeping' arrangements such as break times, finish time, where facilities such as syndicate rooms or toilets are located.

- Make clear to the group there are benefits of effective communication in dealing with difficult or potentially dangerous situations and risks in not paying attention to what and how we communicate.

2. Non-verbal communication

- Explain the importance of non-verbal communication, or body language, in communication as a whole and why it is important to understand it in order to avoid or cope with difficult or violent situations.

See Part One, Chapter 12, pp. 127–131.

- Discuss with the group the possible effects of impressions and stereotypes we all have. Ask them for examples from their own experience to show both the risks and possible advantages of these.

  See Part One, Chapter 12, pp. 128.

- For each of the elements of body language identified in the text (i.e. dress – listening) select a method of conveying to the group its importance and effects in non-verbal communication. For example, in relation to dress, you could show them pictures and ask them about the wearer of the clothes; for facial expression or body posture. You could ask volunteers to demonstrate (as in charades) feelings to the group; for voice you could ask several people to say the same thing in different ways; for listening you could demonstrate the difference between active listening and just being there.

  See Part One, Chapter 12, pp. 128–134.

- Sum up the session by asking the whole group to complete a list of:
  - positive non-verbal communication they could adopt;
  - non-verbal 'danger' signals they will look out for.

  You could have two sub-groups, one working on each list and presenting findings to the whole group.

BREAK – 15 mins

3. Assertiveness – Introduction

- Explain that assertive behaviour is a learned 'positive' behaviour and that it involves recognizing and respecting the rights, feelings, needs and opinions of self and others. It is not about getting your own way all the time

  See Part One, Chapter 9, p. 80 and p. 87.

- For each of the behaviour types in the text (i.e. aggressive, passive, manipulative and assertive) identify with the group:
  - what each behaviour is characterized by;
  - the effects of the behaviour on others.

  You could ask the whole group to identify characteristics and effects initially and then add to it. You could create four sub-groups and ask each of them to take one of the behaviours, identify the characteristics and effects and feed their results back to the whole group where everyone could add to their work; or each sub-group could consider all four behaviour types and then compare results.

  See Part One, Chapter 9, pp. 80–87.

- Summarize the key points that distinguish assertive behaviour as an effective and positive form of communication.

LUNCH – 1 hour

4. Assertiveness – practice

- Explain the rights of individuals and the importance of remembering that we and others have the same rights; also why remembering our rights and those of others is important.

  See pp. 87–88 for 'Rights'.

- For each of the areas of communication (i.e. from Making requests to Feedback), or those most relevant to the group,

  See Part One, Chapter 9, pp. 88–97.

183

explain how to communicate assertively in each area or ask them for their ideas of assertive approaches and add to them through discussion in the group.

- In order to practise assertive communication you could provide roleplay outlines for the group to work through or you could ask them for examples of real life situations from the work setting that they could practise on.

Roleplay could also be done in sub-groups.

- Once the group has had the opportunity to practise, review with them what they have found difficult or easy and identify what are the key points of assertive communication that must be remembered.

You could have more than one review session (e.g. after one or two exercises at a time) or just one review session at the end.

5.   Action plan

Ask each group member to prepare an action plan for themselves outlining what action they will take to implement their learning about:

- non-verbal communication;

- assertive communication.

They may then explain their plan to another group member or a sub-group who could help clarify or expand their plan.

  With the whole group (or those who wish) agree a timetable for further practice of assertive communication.

6.   Summary/evaluation

- Summarize the main learning points from the day either verbally or as a pre-prepared written list - or ask the group to contribute to a list you compile together if time permits.

- Conduct an evaluation using a form or group exercise that will provide information about what the group perceived as:
    - of greatest value;
    - most useful to them at work;
    - should be kept/should be dropped;
    - most/least interesting or enjoyable;
    - well done/not so well done;
    - most/least difficult.

- Explain any further or follow-up evaluation you plan to conduct.

DEVELOPING A POLICY AND PROCEDURES TO COMBAT VIOLENCE AT WORK

Aim

To encourage and enable managers (and others involved) to develop policies and procedures to protect employees from violence.

This programme is written for participants from one organization; it can be adapted for participants from more than one organization.

Notes for trainers

Objectives

At the end of the programme the learners will be able to:

- develop a draft definition of violence relevant in their workplace;

- identify the duties of employers in respect of safety from violence at work;

- identify areas of potential risk within their own organization;

- describe the elements of a policy on violence at work;

- draft a policy for the organization;

- develop procedures necessary to implement the policy.

Time

2 days

Target Groups

Policy makers, managers or others involved in the development of the policy on violence, e.g. personnel staff, health and safety staff, management and employee representatives on health and safety committees.

As programme is highly participative a small number, e.g. 12 works better.

185

Resources

Flipcharts, pens and/or OHP. Handouts and other pre-prepared materials.

Environment

A room large enough for the whole group to work comfortably and space or syndicate rooms for sub-groups. Where managers and policy makers are involved it is as well to be away from the workplace to avoid interruptions.

Timetable

Day 1
1.	Introduction	1 hour
2.	Defining violence at work	1 hour
	BREAK	30 mins
3.	Duties of employers	1½ hours
4.	Identifying risks at work	2 hours
	BREAK	15 mins
5.	Summary/looking forward	¾ hour

Day 2
1.	Introduction	15 mins
2.	Policy development	3½ hours; ½ hr break taken as appropriate
	BREAK	
	Policy development	
	LUNCH	1 hour
3.	Developing procedures	1½ hours
	BREAK	15 mins
4.	Action plans	45 mins
5.	Summary/evaluation	45 mins

Contents

Day 1
1. Introduction

186

Notes for trainers

- Introduce yourself

- Ask the participants to introduce themselves – they will almost certainly know each others' names and roles as they are from the same organization so design an activity to get them to know each other better and start working together.

- Explain any 'housekeeping' arrangements such as start and finish times, break times, where facilities are.

- Using the aims and objectives explain the purpose, content and outcomes of the programme, stressing the practical outcomes for their organization.

- Select key research findings and other information from the text to demonstrate that there is a growing body of evidence that confirms that violence at work is a problem as well as that the problem is on the increase.

  See Part One, Chapter 2, pp. 15–22.

2. Defining violence at work

- Explain to the group what a working definition of violence is, its purpose and why it is important

  Part One, Chapter 1, pp. 12–14.

- Develop a group definition (draft organizational definition) either by:
  - setting sub-groups the task of coming up with a definition and then discussing these in the whole group to come to a group definition. You can then compare with the example in the text and refine if necessary; or
  - showing the group the example working definitions, discuss these and work as a whole group towards a definition that meets their needs and those of their organization.

  See p. 12.

BREAK – 15 mins

3. Duties of employers

  See Part One, Chapter 3, pp. 30–32.

- Pose the group (or sub-groups) the following questions:
  - what are the duties of employers in relation to the safety of staff from violence?
  - what are the costs of not fulfilling the duties?

  Either record the responses of the whole group or get each sub-group to record their answers. If you work with sub-groups ask them to feedback their answers to the whole group.

- Using pre-prepared OHP slides, flipchart or handouts from the text compare the groups' answers to the information in the text:
  - how accurate were they?
  - did they realize the extent of the duties upon them as employers?
  - were they aware of the action that could be taken against them as employers/individuals?
  - did they identify the possible costs to individuals and the organization of not tackling problems of violence to staff?

187

- Ask the group to identify where they feel they do and do not fulfil their duties.

LUNCH – 1 hour

4. Identifying risks at work

See Part One, Chapter 4, pp. 35–40.

- Remind the group of what they said before lunch about how far they believe they do or do not fulfil their duties as employers. Can they be sure if there has been no systematic or thorough investigation?

    Would employees generally share their view?

- Explain the types of activity that have associated risks using the Health and Safety Executive's categories. How many of the organization's activities fit into the categories? What other activities does the organization undertake that may have associated risks?

See p. 35.

- Where to investigate. Explain the idea of an audit as a means of investigating risks. Select a number of areas worth investigating relevant to the particular organization and ask the group members to identify questions or concerns about these areas they would want to investigate.

    Discuss the questions and concerns they identify adding to or amending their lists from the text as appropriate or from the ideas of the rest of the group.

See pp. 35–36.

The group could work individually on areas, or in pairs, trios or larger sub-groups.

- How to investigate. Discuss with the group the questions posed in the text, i.e.
    - What information do you want?
    - What form of information do you want?
    - How much information should you collect?
    - Who should conduct the investigation?

    It is important that they are able to consider these questions before getting into the detail of individual methods.

    For each of the methods of collecting information described in the text:
    - describe it briefly if necessary;
    - ask for views of the advantages and disadvantages of using the method adding information as required;
    - ask the group to say which methods they believe would work best for them and why;
    - ask if they have any other ideas of methods that may work well in the organization or part of it.

See pp. 40–42.

BREAK – 15 mins

5. Summary/looking forward

- Summarize the key learning points from today's sessions either for the group or with them.

Notes for trainers

- Outline the timetable for tomorrow explaining how the work from today links to the work on developing policy and procedure.

Day 2
1. Introduction

Introduce the programme for the day explaining that the purpose of the morning's activities is to produce a draft policy for the organization and the afternoon will focus on developing outline procedures necessary to support the policy. In both these activities they will be drawing on learning from Day 1.

2. Policy development

See Part One, Chapter 5, pp. 48–52.

- Ensure that the group is clear what is meant by a policy and what its purposes are.

- Using the headings from the text identify the areas normally covered by a policy and briefly what each of these covers. These areas may or may not suit the particular organization's requirements so may need to be changed, one or more left out and/or others added. Agree with the group the areas their draft policy will cover.

- The whole group could attempt to draft the whole policy but this may prove very difficult. A more effective approach could be to set up three or four sub-groups each of which takes responsibility for producing a first draft of a number of the policy areas.

These first drafts need to be written up on flipchart or OHP slides or notes copied for everyone.

- Once the sub-groups have completed drafts of their areas of the policy they return to the whole group. In the whole group each policy area, starting at the beginning, can then be taken in turn and discussed, amended, added to or otherwise developed until a final draft is agreed.

A member from each sub-group (or a trainer) will need to take responsibility for noting changes.

- Sub-groups can then write up the final draft of the policy areas they are responsible for.

- Discuss and agree with the group the process for taking the draft policy forward in the organization, eg:
    - who will take responsibility for typing, copying, circulating etc. the draft?
    - who needs to see the draft?
    - what sort of consultation process is necessary?
    - what will be the timescale?
    - who will be responsible for overseeing policy development from here on?

See pp. 48–49.

LUNCH – 1 hour

3. Developing procedures

See Part One, Chapter 5, pp. 52–53.

- The group yesterday identified possible risks at work and have now drafted a policy. The next step is to consider the procedures required to implement the policy and tackle the potential risks of violence they have identified.

They will probably need more information (from an investigation of some sort) in order to be precise about procedures; here they are developing proposals for the procedures they believe are likely to be required.

- Using the examples of the sorts of procedure likely to be required ask the group to identify where they believe the organization needs:
    - to develop new procedures;
    - to change existing procedures;
    - to abandon current procedures.
  Record their responses.

- Once you have a list of their responses help the group to prioritize the needs by identifying, e.g.
    - areas of greatest risk that require urgent attention;
    - actions that can be taken immediately to deal with obvious risks;
    - cost-effective action to which there will be no resistance;
    - changes that may meet with resistance for some reason and will require consultation with or the persuading of others;
    - areas where no action can be taken without further investigation.

- Discuss and agree with the group how their proposals can or will be used:
    - who will be responsible for writing them up/presenting them?
    - to whom should they go?
    - should they accompany the draft policy?
    - should they be kept to a later stage of the policy development process?

BREAK – 15 mins

4. Action plans

- Individuals draw up their own action plan identifying:
    - action they have agreed to take on behalf of the group to further its work on this programme;
    - action they will take immediately in their role to minimize the risk of violence to themselves and others;
    - action they will take individually to further support the development of policy and procedures;
    - action they will take to further develop their own knowledge and skills in relation to combating violence at work;
    - timescales for their actions;
    - help or support they require.

- In pairs, trios or small groups each person takes it in turn to explain their action plan; others can help them, e.g. by adding

Notes for trainers

to the plan, clarifying points, offering support or agreeing to review their progress with them at a later stage.

5. Summary/evaluation

- Summarize the key learning points from the various sessions in the programme with the group or for them, verbally or as written notes.

- Using a form or group exercise evaluate the programme including aspects such as:

content	– appropriateness
	– relevance
	– depth
	– variety
style	– participation/listening
	– active/inactive
time	– length of programme
	– duration of sessions
	– of breaks
materials	– quantity
	– quality
	– range
trainers	– approach
	– confidence with subject
	– presentation
venue	– facilities
	– comfort
	– access
	– refreshments

This type of programme generally takes some time to show its real effects; it is very worthwhile conducting a formal evaluation at a later date or at least monitoring the progress of the participants against their agreed action plans.

PRACTICAL STEPS TO SAFETY

This programme is designed for particular groups of staff with particular needs because of the risks they face, e.g. reception staff, travelling staff, staff who work in others' homes or premises, staff who handle money etc. The first part of the programme is common while the second part of the programme is different depending upon the group being trained.

Aim

To provide participants with practical knowledge of steps they can take to keep safe.

Objectives

At the end of the programme the learners will be able to:

• identify potential areas of risks in their work;

• describe practical steps they can take to keep safe in the course of their work;

• develop an action plan describing the steps they will take
  – to change the way they work;
  – to bring about changes in procedures to ensure safety;
  – to obtain help, support and resources they need.

Time

1 day

Resources

OHP and flipchart and pens, pre-prepared materials and handouts.

Environment

A room large enough for the whole group and space for sub-groups to work or separate syndicate rooms

Timetable

1.	Introduction	30 mins
2.	Violence at work and its effects	30 mins
3.	The risks of violence	1 hour
BREAK		15 mins
4.	Practical session 1	1½ hours
LUNCH		1 hour
5.	Practical session 2	2 hours
BREAK		15 mins
6.	Action plan	30 mins
7.	Summary/evaluation	30 mins

Contents

1. Introduction

- Introduce yourself

- Ask participants to introduce themselves using a name game or similar warm-up exercise.

- Explain the content and outcomes of the programme using the aims and objectives.

2. Violence at work and its effects

See Part One, Chapter 1, pp. 12–14.

- Ask the group what behaviour they would describe as violence at work, including any examples from their experience.

- Show the group the working definitions of violence at work from the text and discuss them, e.g.
    - whether or not they agree with them;
    - if they are wider definitions than they expected;
    - if they cover the areas of behaviour and effects the group think they should.

- Agree a working definition with the group so that everyone is clear about the basis from which the group is working.

193

3. The risks of violence

- Using the research material in the text select examples to illustrate the increasing recognition of violence at work as a problem. Discuss with the group whether they agree with the research findings or not and why they think violence may be on the increase.

See Part One, Chapter 2, pp. 15–22.

- Explain, using figures from the text, the risks of crime. Ask the group if the statistics are what they expected or very different. Ask if they feel they are at risk from crime and, if so, why.

See Part One, Chapter 2, pp. 22–29.

4 and 5. Practical sessions

See Part One, Chapter 10.

These sessions should be designed to meet the needs of the particular group and use the material appropriate to the areas of activity and tasks that the group identifies.

Lunch to be taken at appropriate point.

- Work with the group through the activities and tasks they perform and the way they perform them to identify the risks they face in relation to each.

Do not forget the less obvious aspects of daily work such as travelling to and from work.

- Ask the group for ideas or suggestions as to how they could do their jobs more safely and what support, equipment, resources etc. they need in order to do so. Add to their ideas using materials.

- Depending upon the number of areas of activity or tasks the group identifies, set up sub-groups and ask each group to develop good practice guidelines for one or more of the activities or tasks identified.

- Feed back the good practice guidelines to the whole group adding to them or amending them as the group members contribute their ideas and observations.

BREAK – 15 mins

6. Action plan

- Each individual should identify in their action plans:
  - tasks or activities they will perform differently to minimize any risks to them;
  - support, help, equipment etc. they will try to obtain in order to make their jobs safer;
  - how they will try to bring about any changes in procedure in practice to minimize the risk of violence at work;
  - further information, advice or training they feel they need and how they plan to go about obtaining what they need.

  Ask the group members to try to build in timescales and to find others in the group to support them in achieving their action plan and/or help them assess their progress at an agreed point.

7. Summary/evaluation

- Summarize the key learning points from each of the sessions during the day for the group or ask the group or sub-groups to develop a summary of the sessions for discussion and add to it in the whole group.

- Evaluate the programme to obtain immediate reactions such as:

  - how relevant the group felt it was;
  - if it was practical enough;
  - what more would they have liked;
  - what they would keep the same or change.

  Explain to the group when and how any future evaluation of the programme will take place.

PART FOUR

REFERENCES

BOOKS AND BOOKLETS

Argyle, Michael (1988), *Bodily Communication*, London: Routledge.

Arroba, T. and James, K. (1987), *Pressure at Work: A Survival Guide*, London: McGraw-Hill.

Ashworth, Henry (1981), *Assertiveness at Work*, New York: McGraw-Hill.

Birmingham City Council Women's Unit (1989), *Facing Aggression at Work*, Birmingham City Council (021 235 2549).

Breakwell, G. (1989), *Facing Physical Violence*, London: BPS Books/Routledge.

Davies, Jessica (1990), *Protect Yourself*, London: Judy Piatkus Ltd.

Dickson, Anne (1986), *A Woman in Your Own Right. Assertiveness and You*, London: Quartet Books.

Egan, G. (1990), *The Skilled Helper*, London: Brooks/Cole.

Hanmer, J. and Saunders, S. (1984), *Well-founded Fear – A Community Study of Violence to Women*, London: Hutchinson.

Health and Safety Executive (1990), *A guide to The Health and Safety at Work etc Act 1974*, 4th ed. London: HMSO.

Health and Safety Executive (1988), *Preventing Violence to Staff*, London: HMSO.

Health and Safety Executive (1975), *Health and Safety at Work etc Act, The Act Outlined*, London: Free from HSE.

Lamplugh, Diana (1988), *Beating Aggression – A Practical Guide for Working Women*, London: Weidenfeld and Nicolson.

Lamplugh, Diana (1991), *Without Fear – The Key to Staying Safe*, London: Weidenfeld and Nicolson.

Library Association (1987), *Violence in Libraries*, London: Library Association.

Phillips, C.M. and Stockdale, J.E. (1991), *Violence at Work – Issues, Policies and Procedures*, Luton: Local Government Management Board.

Suzy Lamplugh Trust (1989), *Reducing the Risk – Action Against Violence at Work*, London: Suzy Lamplugh Trust.

ARTICLES

Adcock, J. (1988), 'Prevention of violence to staff', *Local Government Employment*, October.

Brindle, D. (1988), 'Violence against social workers', *Local Government Employment*, June.

Brockington, R. (1989), 'Violence to staff', *Local Government Employment*, August.

Cook, M. (1989), 'A rod for their own backs', *Education*, September.

Copelend, L. (1987), 'Travelling abroad safely: some tips to give employees', *Personnel*, February.

Eaton, L. (1986), 'Lessons on tackling aggression', *Social Work Today*, December.

Eccles, K. and Tuff, N. (1987), 'Defence of the realm', *Insight*, December.

Francis, W. (1986), 'What the organisations say', *Community Care*, December.

Groombridge, B. (1989), 'Risky Work', *Education*, May.

Hall, L. (1989), 'Attacking aggression', *Personnel Today*, May.

Hill, C. (1989), 'Protecting employees from attack', *Personnel Management*, February.

HSIB (1988), 'Preventing violence to staff', *Health and Safety Information Bulletin*, no. 154, October.

Industrial Society Information Service (1989), 'Employers liable for violence to staff', *Industrial Society Magazine*, March.

Lloyd, T. (1989), 'The problem with men', *Social Work Today*, September.

Jervis, M. (1989), 'Wading in at the deep end with a verbal hug', *Social Work Today*, August.

Kelly, B. (1989), 'A case of wolves in sheep's clothing', *Local Government Chronicle*, April.

Painter, K. (1987), 'It's part of the job', *Employee Relations*, vol. 9, no. 5.

Passmore, J. (1989), 'Violent clients – service or safety?', *Housing Planning Review*, vol. 44, no. 2, April/May.

Pugh, R. (1988), 'How to build a system for managing violence', *Social Work Today*, September.

Roberts, M. and Hopkins, J. (1986), 'Confronting violence', *Health Service Journal*, June.

Savery, L. and Gledhill, A. (1988), 'Sexual harassment of women in industry and commerce by co-workers: some Australian evidence', *Personnel Review*, vol. 17, no. 8.

Segal, L. (1989), 'The beast in man', *New Statesman and Society*, September.

Thomas, C. (1987), 'Staff security in housing offices', *Going Local*, no. 7, March. Bristol: SAUS (School for Advanced Urban Studies), Bristol University.

Tonkin, B. (1986), 'Quantifying risk factors', *Community Care*, November.

Whitehead, M. (1988), 'A violent war on the front line', *Local Government Employment*, February.

Wills, J. (1987), 'Realising the risks', *Local Government Chronicle*, November.

Williams, B. and Howe, A. (1988), 'Violence to staff – another possible answer', *Local Government Employment*, February.

REPORTS AND PAPERS

Association of Directors of Social Services (1987), *Guidelines and Recommendations to Employers on Violence against Employees in the Personal Social Services*, ADSS.

Department of Transport (1986), *Assaults on bus staff and measures to prevent such assaults: Report of the working group on violence to road passenger transport staff*, HMSO.

Department of Social Security (1988), *Violence to Staff: Report of the DSS Advisory Committee on Violence to Staff*, HMSO.

Elton Committee (1989), *Discipline in Schools*, Report of the Committee of Enquiry Chaired by Lord Elton, HMSO.

Health and Safety Executive, Health Service Advisory Committee (1988), *Violence to Staff in the Health Services*, HMSO.

Home Office Standing Committee for Violence (1984), *Report of the Working Group – Fear of Crime in England and Wales*, Home Office Public Relations Branch.

Home Office (1989), *Safer Cities – Progress Report 1989–1990*, Home Office Safer Cities Unit.

IDS Study 458 (1990), *Violence against staff*, Income Data Services Ltd.

Labour Research Department (July 1987), 'Assaults on Staff' *Bargaining Report*, pp. 5–12, available from the Labour Research Department.

Phillips,C.M., Stockdale, J.E. and Joeman, L.M. (1989), *The Risks in Going to Work*, Suzy Lamplugh Trust.

Poyner, B. and Warne, C. (1986), *Violence to staff – A basis for assessment and prevention*, Health and Safety Executive.

Rowett, C. (1986), *Violence in social work*, University of Cambridge, Institute of Criminology occasional paper no. 14.

Stott, M. (1988), *Living agenda – Report of a conference at London University on aggression and vulnerability at work*, Suzy Lamplugh Trust.

TUC Report (1987), *Preventing Violence to Staff*, Progress Report, Trades Union Congress.

TUC Report (1988), *Violence to Staff*, Progress Report, Trades Union Congress.

Which Report (November 1990), 'Street Crime', *Which? Magazine* pp. 636–39, Consumers' Association.

TRAINING RESOURCES

Brook Street (1987), *Smart Moves*, Brook Street, St Albans.

Channel 4 Television (1988), *Assert yourself*, Guild Training.

Crown Business Communications (1990), *Well then . . . who is in charge of housing benefit?*, Crown Business Communications.

Leeds Animation Workshop (1983), *Give us a smile*, Leeds Animation Workshop.

Local Government Management Board (1987), *Dealing effectively with aggressive and violent customers*, Local Government Management Board.

Local Government Management Board (1987), *On the front line*, Local Government Management Board.

McGraw-Hill (1982), *Communicating non-defensively – don't take it personally*, McGraw-Hill Films.

Reynolds, N. (1981), *Personal safety*, Rank Aldis.

Social Services Inspectorate (1989), *Violence to staff*, CFL Vision.

Suzy Lamplugh Trust (1989), *Avoiding danger*, Creative Vision.

Suzy Lamplugh Trust (1989), *You can cope – lifeskills training pack*, Gower Publications.

Wiener, R. and Crosby, I. (1986), *Handling violence and aggression*, National Council for Voluntary Child Care Organisation.

The Polytechnic of Wales (1992), a video is currently in production for the use of training students in Chartered Surveying, Estate Management, Land Agency and the Built-in Environment.

Metropolitan Police (1987), *Positive Steps*, Cygnet Films in association with Norwich Union Insurance.

ORGANIZATIONS

British Association for Counselling
37a Sheep Street
Rugby
CV21 3BX
Tel: 0788 78328

British Association of Social Workers
16 Kent Street
Birmingham
B5 6RD
Tel: 021 622 3911

The Home Office
50 Queen Anne's Gate
London
SW1H 9AT
Safer Cities Unit – Room 583a; Public Relations Branch – Room 133

London Rape Crisis Centre
PO Box 69
London
WC1X
Tel: 24hr helpline 071 837 1600; Information 071 278 3959

The Suzy Lamplugh Trust
14 East Sheen Avenue
London
SW14 8AS
Tel: 081 392 1839

Health and Safety Executive
Baynards House
1 Chepstow Place
Westbourne Grove
London
W2 4TF
Tel: 071 221 9178

Commission for Racial Equality
Elliot House
Allington Street
London SW1E 5EH
Tel: 071 828 7022

Equal Opportunities Commission
Overseas House
Quay Street
Manchester M3 3HN
Tel: 071 287 3953 (London)
     061 833 9244 (Head Office Machester)

The Industrial Society
48 Bryanston Square
London W1A 1BQ
Tel: 071 262 2401

Victim Support
Cranmer House
39 Brixton Road
Stockwell
London SW9 5DZ
Tel: 071 735 9166

The Suzy Lamplugh Trust's Programme
for
Reducing the Risks of Violence and Aggression at Work

1. **Guidance for Employers** endorsed by the CBI, written with members of the Health and Safety Executive and other authoritative bodies.

Up-dated and immediately useful information following the Management of Health and Safety at Work Regulations 1992 to help employers comply with their legal obligations to their staff – with the required cooperation of their staff.

2. **Resource Pack** for all places of work, large or small
- Guidance for Employers
- Booklets for all Employees
- Training Resource Manual
- Video of Diana Lamplugh's Talk

3. **Training** by Trust registered trainers to Reduce the Risks of Violence and Aggression at Work.

Plus **Personal Safety First, the Basic Essentials of Personal Safety.** Training by the Trust, or a member of your staff trained as a Personal Safety First Course Tutor, with all the benefits of the Trust's PSF Course Tutor Network.

And many other trainer resources

Write for a brochure from The Suzy Lamplugh Trust, the National Charity for Personal Safety, 14 East Sheen Avenue, London SW14 8AS. Telephone: 0181 392 1839. Fax: 0181 392 1830. Training Office: 0181 876 0305.